THIS
HOMEWARD
ACHE

THIS HOMEWARD ACHE

How Our

Yearning for

the Life to Come

Spurs on Our

Life Today

AMY BAIK LEE

B&H
PUBLISHING
BRENTWOOD, TENNESSEE

978-1-0877-7611-8

Published by B&H Publishing Group
Brentwood, Tennessee

Published in association with Pape Commons,
www.papecommons.com.

Dewey Decimal Classification: 248.84
Subject Heading: CHRISTIAN LIFE / HEAVEN

Cover design by B&H Publishing Group.
Cover image painting Heritage Image Partnership Ltd. /
Alamy Stock Photo. Author photo by Teressa Mahoney.

Portions of this book have been previously published by
the Anselm Society and the Cultivating Project.

1 2 3 4 5 6 • 26 25 24 23

For those who long to live Homeward

Contents

Introduction

It is autumn in the northern hemisphere. Touches of the coming chill have begun to dye honey locust trees yellow and redden the tips of maples. A bittersweet awareness of fleeting glory hangs in the air; an impulse to walk under aspen trees pulls at me as insistently as the attraction of a warm hearth. It's a fitting time, I believe, to write about things that leave us feeling torn in two.

This book is the story of a yearning I encountered before I knew what it was—a yearning that continued even after I discovered its provenance. It remains with me today, and my heart goes out to others I meet who know it.

Some refer to this yearning, this deep and intermittent ache, by the name of *Sehnsucht*. Books both in and out of print discuss it, and many are immensely helpful in spelling out the connection between our longing for an eternal Home and the answering points of the gospel of Jesus Christ.

This book takes a different approach with the same elements. Its aim is not primarily to dissect the experience of Homeward longing but to let the longing rise to the fore, welcoming the bright and fluttering thing for a time so that we might follow it and walk forward with greater faithfulness and joy. This is not a prescriptive work.

Part 1 is written for readers who resonate with this acute longing but haven't found a name for it. I offer the simple things I have to give: the recollection and explorations of a fellow ache-bearer.

Part 2, the main focus of the book, takes the emphasis from Homeward longing into the day-to-day progress of *living* Homeward. These are personal stories, interwoven with ponderings on the kingdom of God and the new creation. Unlike part 1, these essay chapters are not told in chronological order. Homeward longing has radiated outward to affect different areas of my life—like the spokes of a wheel moving out from the center—rather than changing everything in one fell swoop, so each chapter addresses one aspect of "living Homeward."

I've told the stories of part 2 in present tense, in part to lend a tone of immediacy, but mostly to show that they are all still stories in progress. There is a general trajectory to this collection of thirteen readings, which I hope will make itself evident if you choose to read them in order, but please start anywhere you'd like. Altogether, these chapters are for readers who are searching for a "re-enchanted" perspective anchored in God's Word and for weary ones who are trying to hold on to the hope of future wholeness in the face of skepticism, turmoil, and suffering.

At least, those are the lofty aspirations behind this book. The humbler hope at its core is simply to "keep alive in myself the desire for my true country"[1] and hearten my fellow travelers to do the same. I don't have much interest in regaling an audience, but

---

1. C. S. Lewis, *Mere Christianity* (New York: HarperSanFrancisco, 1952, rev. ed. 2001), 137.

it would be an honor to tend the lighthouse flame for someone else who has heard the call of Christ in this way.

This is an ache well worth carrying, friends. The Cause of this longing himself has directed us to "seek the things that are above, where Christ is, seated at the right hand of God" (Col. 3:1). He knows the depth of this pull toward "a better country," lodged in the hearts of his people throughout history, and he "is not ashamed to be called their God, for he has prepared for them a city" (Heb. 11:16).

One day soon our longing will heal in the most curious way, and we will find that it was not a wound that marred our earthly existence, but a cleft through which the fullness of our coming joy shone. And on the day that it breaks open completely, we will finally receive that which we have thirsted to behold and belong to all our lives; like autumn travelers loosed upon a resplendent landscape of beauty with no nightfall ahead, we will find both our peace and our flourishing in the triune Healing of this ache.

Amy Baik Lee
October 2022

PART

1

Homeward
Longing

The sweetest thing in all my life has been the longing—to reach
the Mountain, to find the place where all the beauty came
from—my country, the place where I ought to have been born.
Do you think it all meant nothing, all the longing? The longing for
home? For indeed it now feels not like going, but like going back.

C. S. Lewis, *Till We Have Faces*

Blessed are those whose strength is in you,
in whose heart are the highways to Zion.

Psalm 84:5

1

The Meadow

In the shadow of the Blue Ridge Mountains, on the far eastern outskirts of Boone, North Carolina, a quiet road steals away from the main thoroughfare and winds up a thickly wooded hill. It skirts a line of evergreen sentries before curving and climbing swiftly to a row of weathered mailboxes. The ground slopes downward behind these mailboxes, and if you pause for a minute here, you might spy a little brown house peeking up at you through two shy sash windows set in a gabled wall.

Twenty-nine years ago, I stepped out the front door of this house. The light of a ripening afternoon filtered and winked through the trees, coaxing me outside, and my mother and I meandered up the hill for the first time. Wild raspberry bushes held out bright red gems over the edge of the road. After we nodded to the unruffled cows in the neighboring field and passed three houses, the asphalt turned to plain dirt.

We walked on, up the short rise ahead, and there I saw it.

The left side of our path opened to a wide view of meadows on a hillside, across a slender valley. Sunlight and cloud shadows played upon the distant sea of cropped grass, alert to the whim of the conducting breeze. Clusters of trees rimmed the green and gold expanse; here and there within it a single tree stood alone, its limbs extended in an earthbound dance.

Hidden away from all but a few pairs of eyes, that verdant hill seemed timeless. The air about it still bore the hush of fresh creation, and it met the sky in a curve so gentle and seamless that it might have been the very edge of the world itself.

I had no words to express the yearning that swept through me at that moment. I had no wish to plunge into the forested hollow before me or to climb the hill to the meadow; I only knew that I wanted to stand very still and be enfolded in the rustling quiet of that sight.

Something I had only sensed in times of great grief and great wonder had me in its grasp, and I had no name for it at all.

◇ ◇ ◇

I returned to that spot many times over the next two years, sometimes with my family, sometimes alone on my bicycle. Alone was best, for as much as I was drawn to the view and the recollection of its mark on me, I never wanted to be caught gazing at it for too long; I never wanted to turn and find someone looking at the expression on my face with amused curiosity. In those moments it felt as though a deep tenderness was uncovered, risking ridicule and misunderstanding the longer it lay open.

Once, as I paused for a walking break with my mother, a woman ambled out of a nearby house to say hello. She asked me what I thought of the scenery. Caught off guard, I gestured shyly toward the meadow and said it seemed like heaven.

She laughed. "I never thought of it that way. It *is* pretty, isn't it?" We smiled affably at each other then, and I offered no further comment. At ten years old, I was learning that the sights and sounds I treasured didn't necessarily strike others in the same way.

But the experience of looking at that meadow was the first taste I remember of a longing that would haunt me in the years to come. I stood and lingered at that site of ineffable attraction the way I slowed my pace while reading a new and rivetingly good book in those days. I caught a stronger slip of it every now and again when listening to music, but perhaps it's more accurate to say that it caught me. A keen piercing, a cresting swell, a sudden sheen of tears, and it was gone.

At the time I hadn't the faintest idea that this impression was a glimmer of something that would attend me for the rest of my life. When we moved away, I never thought to take a photograph of that meadow, and I'm now glad I didn't. I would not come again to that spot until more than two decades had passed. But when I left it for the last time, I carried something of it away with me, something that would rise and reawaken much later: the memory of a setting, a stillness, an ache that sank deep down to bide its time and make way for joy of a magnitude I could not have imagined.

2

A Far-off Country

When I was nearly eleven, we moved to Korea. The Appalachian landscape I had known throughout my childhood vanished from my daily view and gave way to the rhythms and sights of metropolitan Seoul.

The way I took in my surroundings seemed to shift along with this change; whether on foot or on public transportation, my mind recorded reels of close-by objects. The free-falling second hand on the wall clock of our neighborhood grocery store. The slick metallic line down the middle of my weekday subway tickets. Saffron-hued ginkgo leaves, their outlines etched onto the sidewalk in a hundred fan-shaped tea stains after an autumn rain. Every nerve in me quickened in response to this bewildering transplantation: a familiar but daunting language with multiple honorific and informal modes, a new school, and daily encounters with strangers of all ages kept me on constant alert, barely able to keep up with all that was happening in the present instant.

But in still moments the nearsighted focus turned inward, and homesickness stood out sharp and clear. I remembered mountains with gentler hues and peaks. I could hear the creak of swings flying high at a Blowing Rock playground at twilight even as I observed the rattling progress of a businessman on his bicycle in the mornings. Our weekly outing to the public library was a thing of the past; as the months wore on, it was hard to remember that there had been such a place.

Relatives and acquaintances asked me if I liked living in Korea better than living in the U.S., and sometimes they went a step further to ask if I missed my old home. Yes, I missed it. I missed visible stars, wild buttercups, chocolate chips, sentences that didn't twist my tongue, and the cherry pits my classmates and I had planted in the schoolyard when the teacher wasn't watching. We were sure they would come up someday.

Yet, even with these concrete images in my mind, there were times when the same intensity of yearning swept in without a connection to anything I knew. I had a growing sense of missing something more than the old house and town and favorite haunts, as if some part of me were aware that the way back was not the way to what I loved most. Somehow, a plane ticket to North Carolina would be as fruitless as the purchase of the meadow would have been on that day long ago.

In the fall semester of that school year, I knelt by the radiator in my small international school classroom and became a Christian. I understood the terms of the rescue that were being offered to me, or I thought I did at the time. I now see I knew as much about what transpired in that moment as a newborn does at birth. From that point on I drank in everything I could learn about this story of faith and its history and its songs, and I began to gain a new view of the world with the help of good mentors and authors.

But the yearning that still pealed sonorously through my days every now and again had no link in my mind to my newfound life in Christ. To tell the truth, anything related to emotions became suspect to me for several years, especially when it came to matters of faith. The missionaries I admired and the biographers who told their stories seemed to think mostly in terms of apologetics, cross-cultural bridges, and sacrificial living, so I followed suit. Meanwhile, the concerns of middle-school friendships and grades and exams occupied my attention, and I unconsciously loosed my hold on the nebulous desire.

A few years later, however, I picked up C. S. Lewis's *Surprised by Joy* and *Weight of Glory* for the first time. I didn't grasp half of what I was reading at first, but I understood that Lewis was writing about a hidden yearning. His account suggested that my own experience might also have theological and philosophical bases—and this idea startled me to the core. Like a long-forgotten scent rising out of old pages came these words:

> In speaking of this desire for our own far-off country, which we find in ourselves even now, I feel a certain shyness. I am almost committing an indecency. I am trying to rip open the inconsolable secret in each one of you—the secret which hurts so much that you take your revenge on it by calling it names like Nostalgia and Romanticism and Adolescence; the secret also which pierces with such sweetness that when, in very intimate

conversation, the mention of it becomes immi-
nent, we grow awkward and effect to laugh at
ourselves; the secret we cannot hide and cannot
tell, though we desire to do both. We cannot tell
it because it is a desire for something that has
never actually appeared in our experience. We
cannot hide it because our experience is constantly suggesting it, and we betray ourselves like
lovers at the mention of a name.[1]

Here was the ache I knew, called out into a clearing. I recognized
this "inconsolable secret." It was a haunting companion to me
already, but Lewis spoke of it in relation to a "far-off country,"
a place yet unreached. How could I so intensely miss a place to
which I had never been?

Lewis introduced a German word for this very idea to me
in his autobiography: *Sehnsucht*.[2] Corbin Scott Carnell, examining the theme of Sehnsucht throughout Lewis's works, defines
it as "the particular attitude which is characterized by a sense of
separation from what is desired, a ceaseless longing which points
always beyond."[3] Rebecca K. Reynolds describes its elusive quality
further:

Sehnsucht is a feeling that you are missing something you love dearly but cannot quite explain to

1. C. S. Lewis, *The Weight of Glory and Other Addresses* (New York:
HarperSanFrancisco, 1949), 29–30.

2. C. S. Lewis, *Surprised by Joy: The Shape of My Early Life* (San Diego:
Harcourt Brace, 1955), 7.

3. Corbin Scott Carnell, *Bright Shadow of Reality: Spiritual Longing in
C. S. Lewis* (Grand Rapids: Eerdmans, 1999), 27.

anyone, not even fully to yourself. It is a yearning for an ideal that floats always in the peripheral vision of your soul, but it disappears every time you turn and try to look at it. *Sehnsucht* is puttering through vulgar, mundane struggles, missing a home you cannot quite reach, and at the same time longing for a far-off land you have never seen. It is wanting to be in a place you cannot name, though whatever "it" is feels familiar. It is wishing to talk to someone dear to you but not knowing who that is. It is desire, but what is desired can't quite be defined.[4]

This was the name I had so plainly lacked on the hillside, and I gradually saw it hadn't left me since then. Scattered instances of the ache, long dormant in my memory, rose *en masse* like a murmuration of reunited starlings. I began to recognize that the moments I kept to myself, the ones that bore an almost debilitating concentration of beauty and peace and poignancy, all belonged to the same species.

But Lewis was also saying something more in the aforementioned passage. According to him, the "far-off country" to which Sehnsucht pointed was solid and *real*, and the more I looked, the more the Word of God acknowledged this was true. The marginalia in my Bible grew as I noted that it referred to its people of faith as "strangers and exiles on the earth" (Heb. 11:13). It exhorted the body of Christ to live different lives because its members

---

4. Rebecca K. Reynolds, *Courage, Dear Heart: Letters to a Weary World* (Colorado Springs: NavPress, 2018), 187–88.

are "refugees from this dying world" (Heb. 6:18 PHILLIPS) and "strangers and 'temporary residents'" (1 Pet. 2:11 PHILLIPS) here. And it did not scorn to call such displaced people its own; of the countless men and women who lived and died looking toward a distant homeland, the writer of Hebrews wrote, "God is not ashamed to be called their God, for he has prepared for them a city" (11:16).

The book of Revelation had captivated me the day I first read of that city, "new Jerusalem, coming down out of heaven from God, prepared as a bride adorned for her husband" (21:2). I knew her arrival would be the beginning of an eternity set in a new heaven and a new earth, and I marveled to read of a time when "death shall be no more, neither shall there be mourning, nor crying, nor pain anymore, for the former things have passed away" (v. 4). As a young Christian I had heard sermons and Bible class lessons about the new Jerusalem; they were scattered among other things, like Old Testament time lines, the legal details of Leviticus, and the birth order of the twelve sons of Jacob. But at the outset of my journey, as I mentioned, I'd never dreamed the promises of my God had any relation to the old ache.

Yet now I began to wonder. If these words were true, could the yearning I felt be the result of my separation from a world that was yet to be, a world to which I already belonged?

Looking at Ephesians 2, Timothy Keller notes that Paul "claims not only that we will *be* resurrected bodily at the end of time but that we have already *been* resurrected spiritually the moment we believed in Christ as our risen Savior and Lord."[5]

---

5. Timothy Keller, *Hope in Times of Fear: The Resurrection and the Meaning of Easter* (New York: Viking, 2021), 118.

From the moment of our acceptance of Christ's salvation and lordship, we begin to breathe the reality of a new life:

> We begin to experience foretastes of our final future state—a freedom to change and be like Christ, a sense of God's reality, glory, and love in our hearts, and a new, loving solidarity with brothers and sisters in Christ.
>
> Spiritual resurrection means that we are, in a sense, living in heaven while still on earth, living in the future while still being in the present.[6]

The longing to be fully in that final state, then, may be the sanest possible reaction a Christian can have. What could be more natural than to feel a pull toward one's home? G. K. Chesterton describes the relief he once felt when he encountered the odd, "optimistic" Christian view of the world:

> The modern philosopher had told me again and again that I was in the right place, and I had still felt depressed even in acquiescence. But [then] I had heard that I was in the *wrong* place, and my soul sang for joy, like a bird in spring. The knowledge found out and illuminated forgotten chambers in the dark house of infancy. I knew now why grass had always seemed to me as queer as the green beard of a giant, and why I could feel homesick at home.[7]

---

6. Keller, *Hope in Times of Fear*, 118–19.
7. G. K. Chesterton, *Orthodoxy* (New York: Doubleday, 1959), 80.

Ah. Like Chesterton, I had accepted the changes, the adjustments, and the transience of my location in the world and found that almost everything fit tidily into the closed book of acquiescence, except this one quivering, indelible gleam. It caught on everything.

Knowing that I was bound for a destination that would satisfy this hidden hunger—a destination that was *responsible for the hunger in the first place*—changed the tenor of my longing completely. I understood now that the old ache dappled an entire terrain that lay between the present hour and a promised home to come. The myopic view of my childhood widened, but instead of evaporating, the ache deepened and spread. My Sehnsucht became a yearning with a path forward and a known destination.

3

A Yearning with a Destination

When I packed my suitcase to leave Korea in 2001, I didn't know where my footsteps would go over the next decade. In that span of time, I would finish my senior year of high school in southwestern Virginia, attend college and graduate school in central Virginia, and finally fly to Colorado with my husband of three years and our first baby on the way.

With each move—some of them within the bounds of the same town—a noticeable pattern began to emerge. Every new place started out as a haphazard constellation, a smattering of locations in the blank pages of my mental atlas. A "You Are Here" point anchored the map in my current apartment first, and over time, as I came upon a certain coffee shop or local landmark, the map in my mind filled out with distinct features. It always took me about a year to understand how they all connected; I learned that I could see the treetops of that street from this rise or that I could get home fifteen minutes sooner by taking that local road. The more my knowledge of the surrounding community grew, the more I came to understand the character and context of where I was.

The same thing has happened as I've explored Sehnsucht and its close relatives, and it is probably wise to roll out and share this map before I explain further what "Homeward longing" means to me. Lewis noted how easy it is to conflate Sehnsucht with other thoughts and impressions. "I still believe that the experience is common, commonly misunderstood, and of immense importance," he wrote, "but I know now that in other minds it arises under other stimuli and is entangled with other irrelevancies and that to bring it into the forefront of consciousness is not so easy as I once supposed."[1] I've found this to be true in my own life and have had to sift and distinguish Sehnsucht from other "stimuli and irrelevancies" in order to move forward with it.[2]

Sehnsucht

Sehnsucht itself is astonishingly more common than I once thought. From around the world, the Welsh word *hiraeth* and the Portuguese and Brazilian *saudade* are frequently mentioned as approximate synonyms; others have proposed the Galician *morriña*, Romanian *dor*, Ethiopian *tizita,* and Korean *galmang.*

---

1. C. S. Lewis, afterword to *The Pilgrim's Regress: An Allegorical Apology for Christianity, Reason, and Romanticism* (Grand Rapids: William B. Eerdmans, 2014), 234.
2. Many of these words are moving targets in contemporary language. I've found that what one person means by "nostalgia" may be exactly what I mean by Sehnsucht, and what another calls "homesick for heaven" may have very little to do with the subject matter of this book. I've tried to make my own distinctions as clear as possible here for the sake of the chapters that follow.

All of these terms seem to come with the same caveat whenever they're discussed: "The essence of this longing can't really be translated," someone will say. But Svetlana Boym, in her extensive study *The Future of Nostalgia*, notes that this very caveat is shared internationally:

> While each term preserves the specific rhythms of the language, one is struck by the fact that all these untranslatable words are in fact synonyms; and all share the desire for untranslatability, the longing for uniqueness. While the details and flavors differ, the grammar of romantic nostalgias all over the world is quite similar.[3]

The "details and flavors" of these "nostalgias" are indeed beautifully varied. In some cultures, the acknowledgment of this experience is so widely shared that popular creative expressions emerge, like the musical theme of saudade in Portuguese fado music.

But if Boym is right and there is indeed a shared telltale "grammar" to all these words, I suspect the commonality goes deeper than a desire to stand apart; I believe it stems from the instinctive knowledge that what lies at the core of *saudade* and *dor* and *Sehnsucht* cannot be packaged up neatly. Even within a primary language, we grasp for words to describe the ache; it is not easily translated because it is not easily defined.

Yet one consistent mark of this longing that surfaces across the world is, strangely, its attractiveness. There's a sweetness in it that makes it worth harboring or even seeking out. Lewis

---

3. Svetlana Boym, *The Future of Nostalgia* (New York: Basic Books, 2001), 13.

describes it as an "acute and even painful" desire that somehow feels delightful; "even when there is no hope of possible satisfaction, [it] continues to be prized, and even to be preferred to anything else in the world, by those who have once felt it."[4] Hence, the word Lewis chooses for his discussion of Sehnsucht is *Joy*. As Alan Jacobs points out, "The word *longing* fails to convey the desirability of the feeling itself. No one, presumably, wants to be in a state of longing, but anyone would want to experience Joy."[5]

This "Joy" is no mere synonym for happiness, and it resonates with my experience of this yearning too. The word draws from the same nuanced range as J. R. R. Tolkien's phrase, "a fleeting glimpse of Joy, Joy beyond the walls of the world, poignant as grief."[6] Poignancy, grief, delight, pain—this is a longing that plumbs our depths.

In L. M. Montgomery's *Anne's House of Dreams*, Anne Blythe—née Shirley—contemplates the many dimensions of this joy with a friend one evening:

> Silence and twilight fell over the garden. Far away the sea was lapping gently and monotonously on the bar. The wind of evening in the poplars sounded like some sad, weird, old rune—some broken dream of old memories. A slender shapely young aspen rose up before them against the fine maize and emerald and paling

---

4. Lewis, afterword to *Pilgrim's Regress*, 234.

5. Alan Jacobs, *The Narnian: The Life and Imagination of C. S. Lewis* (New York: HarperOne, 2005), 41.

6. J. R. R. Tolkien, "On Fairy-Stories," in *Tree and Leaf*, rev. ed. (London: HarperCollins, 2001), 69.

rose of the western sky, which brought out every leaf and twig in dark, tremulous, elfin loveliness.

"Isn't that beautiful?" said Owen, pointing to it with the air of a man who puts a certain conversation behind him.

"It's so beautiful that it hurts me," said Anne softly. "Perfect things like that always did hurt me—I remember I called it 'the queer ache' when I was a child. What is the reason that pain like this seems inseparable from perfection? Is it the pain of finality—when we realise that there can be nothing beyond but retrogression?"

"Perhaps," said Owen dreamily, "it is the prisoned infinite in us calling out to its kindred infinite as expressed in that visible perfection."[7]

Though he speaks sentimentally, Owen Ford's brief reflection touches on something that mankind has long sensed. The book of Ecclesiastes states more overtly that God "has put eternity into man's heart" (3:11); our "prisoned infinite," bound by time and mortality, calls out to the "kindred infinite" that currently lies beyond its reach.

The beauty that hurts, this exquisite pain weighted with solemnity and wonder, is thus a joy steeped in longing and a longing steeped in joy; our sense of separation from eternity brings both the relief and the pang of knowing that things are not as they should be. But there, I'm getting ahead of myself.

---

7. L. M. Montgomery, *Anne's House of Dreams* (Toronto: McClelland and Stewart, 1922), 188.

Setting Sehnsucht beside the following experiences has helped me see its distinctiveness.

Nostalgia

Nostalgia, in spite of its old-world roots, is a relatively new term. In 1688, a Swiss doctor named Johannes Hofer put the Greek words *nostos* and *algos* together to speak of a kind of "homecoming pain," a debilitating condition that involved physical symptoms and seemed to be cured by a return to one's native land. Since then, nostalgia has had a long and fraught history with societal responses ranging from sympathy to scorn.

I believe the original cobbled-together meaning of nostalgia strikes fairly close to Sehnsucht: "heartache for the homecoming," as Anthony Esolen phrases it.[8] But the word has long since petered off into a more wistful connotation.

To me, nostalgia is an affectionate longing for a setting that is located in the past, like the baby stage of my daughters' lives or the study dates I used to have with my best friend. It can reach a pitch of intensity that prods me to sit down until the wave of memory subsides.

Still, when I'm struck by nostalgia, I know what I'm missing, which is why the burden lightens when I am able to get together and reminisce with others who shared the same setting. Nostalgia is thus more focused in scope than Sehnsucht.

What is more, if I go back honestly to the pleasant pictures of the past, I usually remember that things were never as simple as

---

8. Anthony Esolen, introduction to *Nostalgia: Going Home in a Homeless World* (Washington, DC: Regnery Gateway, 2018), xxi.

the fond fragments I've retained. And frequently, the best memories, the sweetest ones that bear up under scrutiny, have a flash of longing embedded in them that I felt even as I lived the original scene. Nostalgia may direct my gaze backward in time, but Sehnsucht often catches it and directs it toward something more fulfilling and complete, something of which the former time gave only a hint.

Homesickness

If nostalgia looks back to a past time or condition, homesickness generally looks to a physical *place*, or, sometimes, to the remnants of that place. It can be a gracious pain, a reminder that we have had the privilege of anchoring our memories and growing into a sense of belonging somewhere.

"I miss the sea,"[9] says Sarah Wheaton in *Sarah, Plain and Tall*. She longs for her seaside home and her brother and her three old aunts "who all squawk together like crows at dawn,"[10] even as she tries out the idea of establishing a new life and a new family on the prairie. The specifics matter to her, as they do to all who are homesick, including the blue, gray, and green shades of the sea she brings home in colored pencils.

When we are fortunate, a past home is a casement through which we may glimpse the healing welcome of a future one. Frederick Buechner writes, "I believe that what we long for most in the home we knew is the peace and charity that, if we were

9. Patricia MacLachlan, *Sarah, Plain and Tall* (New York: Scholastic, 1985), 40.

10. MacLachlan, *Sarah, Plain and Tall*, 40.

lucky, we first came to experience there, and I believe that it is that same peace and charity we dream of finding once again in the home that the tide of time draws us toward."[11] Homesickness can thus give us a greater capacity to recognize, celebrate, and hope for a Home we have not seen.

Still, Sehnsucht and homesickness—as we tend to use the word—are not one and the same. Both can be formidable; both can be triggered by sights, sounds, and other stimuli. But frequently the distinguishing factor between the two seems to be a restlessness, inherent in Sehnsucht, that cannot be sated by the places we know.

I've encountered that difference in my own life. Once, in Korea, a song I listened to while looking out of a ninth-floor balcony spoke of a rootedness and continuity greater than my seasons of change; another time, in Virginia, I rounded a corner in an apartment soon after moving in and found the table drenched in a torrent of morning light that stopped me where I stood. Both times a tug as powerful as homesickness took hold, but both times I was *at home*. Something more enduring than the song and the scene called to me in a way that was familiar but foreign—exquisite but inscrutable.

Melancholy

The state of melancholy can also be offered as an explanation for Sehnsucht, if one believes the yearning rises from a particular personality.

---

11. Frederick Buechner, introduction to *Longing for Home: Recollections and Reflections* (New York: HarperSanFrancisco, 1996), 3.

Melancholy was, as the ancient Greeks believed, one of four humors in the human body that affected health and temperament. Their theories on these fluid humors influenced later studies on personality and remain preserved in the word we use for melancholy today: *melan* ("black") and *kholē* ("bile"). The melancholic temperament in literature can range from Philippa Gordon's "a little blue—just a pale, elusive azure"[12] to Hamlet, who contends that the blackest suits and moods of mourning would not be enough to convey "that within which passes show."[13] I tend toward the melancholic end of the personality spectrum naturally; at the end of each year, a streaming music service tells me that my default listening preferences are incurably "mellow" and "wistful."

But from where I stand, melancholy lacks the searching quality of Sehnsucht. "Melancholy is the pleasure of being sad,"[14] Victor Hugo averred, and I agree; it is a blanketing pensive stillness, an inward-dwelling state of mind. I do not think it is quite fair to dub it emotional for the sake of being emotional; the melancholic mood can lay the necessary groundwork for acknowledging pain or accepting rest from exhaustion. But melancholy is more of a hovering than a reaching, and thus more prone to sink a person into the lightless depths of depression or despair if he stays within it for too long. Moments of Sehnsucht are different; here one may also dwell for a time, especially to soak in whatever has triggered the yearning, but Sehnsucht soon rouses its bearer

---

12. L. M. Montgomery, *Anne of the Island* (New York: Signet Classic, 1991), 43.

13. William Shakespeare, *Hamlet*, 1.2.88. Reference is to act, scene, and line.

14. "La mélancolie, c'est le bonheur d'être triste." Victor Hugo, *Les Travailleurs de la mer* (Brussels, 1866).

to look in the direction of the source. It lifts one's gaze not further downward but outward and upward.

An Appreciative Regard for Beauty

Encounters with beauty, too, are sometimes equated with Sehnsucht. I believe there is an approach to beauty that is relevant to the yearning, which I'll bring up later in this book, but what some mean by "an appreciation for beauty" is a pleasantness akin to strolling through a well-appointed exhibit at a museum: an aesthetic tickle. If we take that tickle and dial it up in potency, they suggest, we might bring forth a reaction so strong that it can be labeled as longing.

But Lewis, noticing our tendency to conflate the two, clarifies that Sehnsucht is not found *in* but *beyond* beauty:

> Our commonest expedient is to call it beauty and behave as if that settled the matter. . . . [But] the books or the music in which we thought the beauty was located will betray us if we trust to them; it was not *in* them, it only came *through* them, and what came through them was longing. . . . For they are not the thing itself; they are only the scent of a flower we have not found, the echo of a tune we have not heard, news from a country we have never yet visited.[15]

---

15. C. S. Lewis, *The Weight of Glory and Other Addresses* (New York: HarperSanFrancisco, 1949), 30–31.

If beauty is a channel, it cannot be the cause. I believe Lewis is right. Beauty can spark Sehnsucht, but one can encounter Sehnsucht without any vestige of conventional beauty in sight. They are not interchangeable.

Escapism

Finally, it seems plausible that Sehnsucht could arise from being locked in less-than-ideal circumstances. What could make more sense than trying to find significance in a difficult time by nurturing a yearning for something good, even transcendent? Could it be that Sehnsucht is just our mental escape hatch for the darkest of days?

I am neither a psychologist nor a philosopher, but the door of Sehnsucht does not seem to be marked with an exit sign. The yearning has come not only in the trenches of my life but also on the peaceful plateaus. Regarding the former, it usually offers no solution for my current problems. If a good escape is supposed to provide a means of getting away from a burden or a snare, Sehnsucht seems to work in the opposite way; it draws one not *away* from but *toward* a specific destination.

One may find plenty of accounts, fictional and historical, of people dreaming of escape in various situations, but not so many of people dreaming of being surprised by Sehnsucht; the latter is a force that comes almost despite ourselves. In escapism we reach out; in Sehnsucht, something else breaks in.

◊ ◊ ◊

Nostalgia, homesickness, melancholy, the appreciation of beauty, and even escapism are part of the landscape of human experience, and they weave through it like streams, good for dipping one's feet in for refreshment or remembrance, helpful for the occasional washing of wounds.

But they are each, by themselves, incomplete. Each stream has at one point or another drawn me further into the deeper waters of Sehnsucht. Other times, I've indulged the emotions behind them and wandered along the banks of each kind of desire, following watery offshoots until they trickle into nothingness and my sense of direction dries up. While stumbling back, I have observed that these smaller longings can act as tributaries leading to a greater river, but the greater river itself does not flow back into *them*.

Yet even the analogy of a river is inadequate, for the yearning that drew me out the door of familiarity is not a fixed and visitable location on my map. If anything, Sehnsucht is far more like a strong current running at the center of all these longings, or a glint of sea on the horizon, or an unexplained rush of wind in the close quarters of an upper room. Something calls, and some counterpart in me, rejoicing, wakes up.

There's still a great deal of blank space in my cartographic understanding of this yearning, and there are certainly broader and finer ideas explored by others that I will never know in full. But just as dots and lines on a map begin to take on personal meaning, like a hilly tree-lined street here in Colorado that reminds me of the Virginia countryside, or the "H" sign marking the way to the hospital where my children were born, so too this invisible feature of Sehnsucht-joy has taken on a special identity to me.

In the history told by the Scriptures that I've read since my prayer by the classroom window, the act of renaming has always signaled a paradigm shift: Sarai to Sarah, Luz to Bethel, Simon to

Peter. And in a change much smaller but perhaps no less momentous, Sehnsucht has been christened anew for me as I look to my eventual arrival in that far-off country:

I live with a Homeward longing.

4

Pierced by Peace

H omeward longing" is the name I've quietly given for personal reference to this ache, this intersection where Sehnsucht meets the Christian view of reality. The narrative centered around the life, death, and resurrection of Christ is still the most comprehensive explanation I've found for the root and the intensity of my yearning. It confesses that there was a great breakage in the past between humankind and its Maker, with shattering echoes that stretch into the present, but it also offers a new beginning through the Person and the redemptive sacrifice of the Son of God. It reveals that we dwell in the great promise of a coming restoration.

"We all long for [Eden], and we are constantly glimpsing it: our whole nature at its best and least corrupted, its gentlest and most humane, is still soaked with the sense of 'exile,'" J. R. R. Tolkien once wrote to his son Christopher.[1] The whole progress

---

1. J. R. R. Tolkien to Christopher Tolkien, Oxford, January 30, 1945, in *The Letters of J. R. R. Tolkien,* eds. Humphrey Carpenter and Christopher Tolkien (Boston: Houghton Mifflin, 2000), 110.

of humankind is rife with this sense of separation, beginning with the first twinges of willful distrust within the first man and woman, coursing down to the inner stirrings of my own heart here in the twenty-first century.

Looking over the span of Scripture, Keller sees the same theme: "It is no coincidence that story after story contains the pattern of exile. The message of the Bible is that the human race is a band of exiles trying to come home."[2] Following this thread through, Keller notes that when the way of homecoming was opened for this "band," it came at an unfathomable cost:

> Jesus had not come to simply deliver one nation from political oppression, but to save all of us from sin, evil, and death itself. He came to bring the human race Home. Therefore he did not come in strength but in weakness. He came and experienced the exile that we deserved. He was expelled from the presence of the Father, he was thrust into the darkness, the uttermost despair of spiritual alienation—in our place. He took upon himself the full curse of human rebellion, cosmic homelessness, so that we could be welcomed into our true home.[3]

In other words, the owner of the Home I seek became an exile in my place. He was pierced for my transgressions and crushed for

---

2. Timothy Keller, *The Prodigal God: Recovering the Heart of the Christian Faith* (New York: Penguin, 2008), 97–98.

3. Keller, *The Prodigal God*, 101–2.

my iniquities (Isa. 53:5), that I might enter into his family as a daughter, an heir jubilantly expected at Home.

On some days, I still find it astounding that the exilic yearning itself is not a helpless diagnosis with a terminal end. Why shouldn't it be the end of the story? What kind of grace is this, that Christ has not only redeemed me but embedded a shard of unsettledness within me so that I would look for its source?

Owe Wikström, a Swedish theologian and professor of religious psychology, tells of a conversation he once struck up with an American priest in Paris.[4] The priest himself was a former neurochemist and art gallery owner, no stranger to "the fundamental feeling of being lost," and he lit his pipe as he exhaled his views:

> The anxiety that comes with life's crises cannot be reduced to sentimentality or regressive tendencies. It is a real feeling, just as tangible as the longing for one's lover or children—who have gone away for a while—is a witness to the fact that they actually exist. The longing is a sign that the other exists. It is the same thing here. The longing is a consequence of man's search for meaning, his ontological thirst. Outside Eden man has become disorientated. Therefore, that which from a human perspective seems in the beginning to be a general state of melancholy or fear of death and from a normal point of view

---

4. While I hold a Reformed Protestant perspective, in this book I've quoted writers and thinkers outside my line of Christian tradition whose insights have helped me look to Christ on this journey Home.

can be interpreted as "a search for meaning," is
in fact God's own action on the human heart.[5]

The priest's pilgrimage arose from his search for meaning, but he highlights a peculiar point of grace that I recognize from my own first brush with joy in the meadow: before I knew God, incredibly, he called to me. Christ's choice to lay his life down so that we strangers and exiles might in the end arrive home to him—this is news from which I hope never to recover. But his initiative in giving us hearts that thirst for and tug us toward the glimmers of the place he has prepared, that we might draw closer to him day by day—the love in this staggers me to no end.

And so my old longing hasn't faded. Is it surprising that it has stayed? I've found that approximate descriptions of Sehnsucht are sometimes met with knowing nods among believers. "You're homesick for heaven. The answer you're searching for is Jesus, of course." Case closed.

But to me this is a bit like saying, "Ah, so you've discovered brilliant dashes of colored light scattered across your living room. It's quite simple: those are rainbows." So they are, and I sometimes pause to watch a scattered cloud of these tiny, many-hued stars as they cross my walls in the spring and summer afternoons. Rainbows they are, indeed. But I have further questions for such a pragmatic speaker. Have you ever stopped to consider the combination of factors necessary to bring them into being? Have you seen the wild weaving whirl they make when the prism in the window spins? Can we set them dancing on a cloudy day? What does

---

5. Owe Wikström, *The Icon in My Pocket: On Outer and Inner Journeys,* trans. Yvonne King (Leominster, UK: Gracewing, 2008), 141.

it say about our perception that light holds so many visible and invisible shades, and who first imagined such an arresting sight, and what does this reveal about the bearer of that imagination, and can we expect more displays of profligate beauty? What does this abundance indicate about the heart of such a Maker?

In short: yes, I believe this deep-set longing in the soul comes from God and that it leads to an imperishable Home. Yet all the surprises I've seen since I met him—the keen shots of delight and solace and startling help—have pierced me more, not less, as I move closer to seeing him in full.

Compunctio: Pierced by Peace and Wholeness

Piercing is a word I try to use sparingly to describe Homeward longing, mostly because I suspect I'd become a one-word writer if I gave it free rein. This ache is undeniably a sharp-edged joy—a sweet pain, as others have said. I've often wondered at the sheer number of instances I've had when the only appropriate word seemed to be "piercing."

But through another of Wikström's encounters with thinkers—this time a French physician-nun—I've also learned that this word relates to a discussion that has been taking place in the church since the Middle Ages. The physician mentions a kind of pain that isn't purely physiological: "the bitter-sweet pain on the borders of joy and sorrow," a pain that "overwhelms man in the middle of a poignant moment of beauty. . . . Where do these tears come from?"[6]

---

6. Wikström, *The Icon in My Pocket*, 136.

She ventures an answer herself: "Gregory the [G]reat spoke of *compunctio*—holy anguish. The sorrow which some feel when confronted with the most beautiful is at the same time a reminiscence of and a foretaste of the divine world."[7]

Compunctio. Oh, the very sound of the word for this "holy anguish" resonates with me even before I go to look it up in the dictionary. *Compunctio* comes from *compungere*: "to prick severely; to sting."[8] And so it does.[9]

In my encounters with Homeward longing in recent years, I've started to notice that an unexpected element frequently accompanies the sting.

In 2019, I attended the evensong of a conference on the re-enchantment of the Christian imagination. The service included Scripture readings, congregational hymns from the church through the ages, a prayer for artists, passages of poetry and short fiction, and a choir made up of conference attendees who had practiced Ennio Morricone's "Gabriel's Oboe" through the lunch

---

7. Wikström, *The Icon in My Pocket*, 136.

8. *The Compact Edition of the Oxford English Dictionary* (1971), s.v. "compunctio."

9. Gregory the Great, an early Church Father, considered there to be four modes of compunction: (1) the compunction of thinking upon one's own sins, (2) the compunction of fearing God's deserved judgment, (3) the compunction of sorrowfully considering the evils of one's present life, and (4) the compunction of thinking of one's heavenly country and yearning for what is not yet (Gregory the Great, *Morals on the Book of Job by St. Gregory the Great*, trans. John Henry Parker, J. G. F. and J. Rivington, 1844, Book XXIII, Volume III—The Fifth Part, accessed February 27, 2023, http://www.lectionarycentral.com/GregoryMoralia/Book23.html). C. S. Lewis's words seem to reflect this fourth kind of piercing when he describes the mark of authentic Sehnsucht or Joy: "It must have the stab, the pang, the inconsolable longing" (C. S. Lewis, *Surprised by Joy: The Shape of My Early Life* [San Diego: Harcourt Brace, 1955], 72).

hour. I knew many of the two hundred or so faces in the room by name. As I write this, I can hear Michelle Drake reading Oscar Wilde's "The Selfish Giant," Terri Moon skillfully drawing harmonic notes from her violin, and Christina Brown's silvery voice leading the final hymn.

I was there to soak up what I could from this "Offering of Beauty" service while my husband picked up our children from a friend's house and took them home to bed. It was a generous gift of time, and I was grateful for it. I had been grappling with symptoms of a chronic illness that would not be diagnosed for another year, and our family was in the midst of helping my father-in-law walk the long goodbye of dementia. For a moment, I let down my guard and my layers of crisis preparedness. I sat in a row next to dear friends and heard their voices ring beside mine in the glad confession of Psalm 19; I looked and listened and exhaled. As the contributions of the evening unfolded, each reader, singer, and dancer seemed to have been made to bring the specific portion they shared.

Gradually, an immeasurable peace mantled my shoulders. Nothing had changed situationally, but I felt unshakably surrounded on every side. In that space of worship, I had a sense that the worst of my fears could happen—whatever the worst might be—and none of it would be able to change the fact of my belonging or the fact of the indomitable goodness of God. As that impression intensified, the relief in that hour was so strong, the beauty so palpable, that toward the end I buried my face in the ends of my scarf and wept. A concentrated, indeed, a *piercing* peace had surprised me, and it surprises me still.

The *compunctio* of joy, of Sehnsucht, of Home, is frequently tinged with this peace. It is as if the veil between this time-bound world and eternity is punctured and, just for a minute, we can see through to the place where there shall be no "mourning, nor crying, nor pain anymore" (Rev. 21:4). We behold a glimpse of a world, *this* very world, whole and unbroken and made new.[10]

Such glimpses can come anywhere, it seems. Buechner shares a memory of a time he went to Sea World with his family and was deeply moved by the motion of orcas on a clear summer day. "[I]t was as if the whole creation—men and women and beasts and sun and water and sky and, for all I know, God himself—was caught up in one great, jubilant dance of unimaginable beauty. And then, right in the midst of it, I was astonished to find that my eyes were filled with tears."[11] His frank thoughts on his reaction spell out what it is to have eternity in our hearts:

---

10. Theologian Herman Bavinck walks through Scripture to suggest that the *substance* of this world will not be destroyed. "Old Testament prophecy, while it looks for an extraordinary transformation in all of nature, refrains from teaching the destruction of the present world. . . . In the same way the New Testament proclaims that heaven and earth will pass away (Matt. 5:18; 24:35; 2 Pet. 3:10; 1 John 2:17; Rev. 21:1), that they will perish and wear out like clothing (Heb. 1:11), dissolve (2 Pet. 3:10), be burned with fire (2 Pet. 3:10), and be changed (Heb. 1:12). But none of these expressions implies a destruction of substance. . . . God's honor consists precisely in the fact that he redeems and renews the same humanity, the same world, the same heaven, and the same earth that have been corrupted and polluted by sin. Just as anyone in Christ is a new creation in whom the old has passed away and everything has become new (2 Cor. 5:17), so this world passes away in its present form as well, in order out of its womb, at God's word of power, to give birth and being to a new world" (Herman Bavinck, *The Last Things: Hope for This World and the Next,* ed. John Bolt, trans. John Vriend [Grand Rapids: Baker Books, 1996], 156–57).

11. Frederick Buechner, *Longing for Home: Recollections and Reflections* (New York: HarperSanFrancisco, 1996), 126.

Joy is home, and I believe the tears that came to our eyes were more than anything else homesick tears. God created us in joy and created us for joy, and in the long run not all the darkness there is in the world and in ourselves can separate us finally from that joy, because whatever else it means to say that God created us in his image, I think it means that even when we cannot believe in him, even when we feel most spiritually bankrupt and deserted by him, his mark is deep within us. We have God's joy in our blood.[12]

We have God's joy in our blood. Our instinctive recognition of a reality beyond our immediate surroundings is affirmed by Canadian author L. M. Montgomery, who remarked that her love of nature brought it to the fore.

It has always seemed to me, ever since early childhood, that, amid all the commonplaces of life, I was very near to a kingdom of ideal beauty. Between it and me hung only a thin veil. I could never draw it quite aside, but sometimes a wind fluttered it and I caught a glimpse of the enchanting realm beyond—only a glimpse—but those glimpses have always made life worth while.[13]

Like Buechner and Montgomery, I know these glimpses are fleeting. At times I stand stricken by their brevity and the contrast

---

12. Buechner, *Longing for Home*, 128.
13. L. M. Montgomery, *The Alpine Path: The Story of My Career* (New York: Start Publishing, 2012), OverDrive.

they make against life at present, but more often than not, they fuel a growing sense of hope. For despite the rending they cause, they confirm that what I've heard and tasted and seen of the love of God is no illusion. "And though you have never seen him, yet I know that you love him," Peter writes in his first epistle, in words that gladden me deeply with their empathy. "At present you trust him without being able to see him, and even now he brings you a joy that words cannot express and which has in it a hint of the glories of Heaven; and all the time you are receiving the result of your faith in him—the salvation of your own souls" (1 Pet. 1:8–9 PHILLIPS).

Altogether, this ongoing ache has changed the direction and the manner of my living. I hold the deposit of the Holy Spirit as a guarantee of all that is to come (2 Cor. 1:21–22; 5:5; Eph. 1:13–14), and I am finding that every nook in this life has influences from and implications in an unseen realm—that everything, to borrow the words of George MacDonald, "is an affair of the spirit."[14]

And as I learn to follow the "hints of glory" as one who has been called rather than one who has conjured, I sometimes find myself bereft of words again. But this time the tender speechlessness rises precisely because I know where I am: in the presence and the keeping of One who was pierced "for the joy that was set before him" (Heb. 12:2). The One who has opened the way for all who desire to come Home to him.

---

14. George MacDonald, "The Cause of Spiritual Stupidity," in *Unspoken Sermons Series Two*, accessed February 27, 2023, https://www.gutenberg.org /cache/epub/9057/pg9057.html.

5

Return to the Meadow

The year I turned thirty-three, I went back to Boone. My parents happened to be working there for a few months, and my husband and I decided that autumn would be the best time of year to take our two little daughters for a visit.

Boone, of all places, has been preserved in ways that other landmarks in my life have not. The international school I attended in Seoul no longer exists. A city has sprouted up around the apartment where I lived in Korea, changing the landscape so drastically that I could no longer recognize the view from my room the last time I visited. The gym roof of the high school I graduated from in Virginia collapsed under two feet of snow twelve years ago; the entire building was subsequently condemned. My college dorm has been demolished, and its old brick walls are no longer there to recount to me those first exhilarating and bewildering tastes of independent life.

But in this small town in North Carolina, many of the roads and buildings are just as they were when I was a foot shorter.

How shockingly familiar everything was when we took the winding mountain route into the valley where I used to live! Without
warning, I was suddenly an elementary school student again,
watching treetops blur by the window, sitting up in anticipation
of an after-school snack—as if the earth hadn't revolved and a
thousand paths hadn't passed beneath my feet since then. That
October, I watched my children play in the mulched school playground where I had spent every recess, and I wondered at the
enigmatic twists of time.

One afternoon, my husband and I left the girls in the care of
my parents and embarked on a long-awaited little pilgrimage—
"long-awaited," that is, in my case. Not knowing how to explain,
I had only casually mentioned to Yongwon that I wanted to visit
the little brown house where I had lived as an older child.

We laughed as the slope of the hill pressed us both back in our
seats on the way up. Yongwon parked on the side of the road. "Is
this the house?" he asked. I nodded.

A tall hedge of shrubbery lined the road, but between the
sparse branches we could see the house. As we stood in front of
the mailboxes, a minivan pulled into the driveway—now covered
by a carport—and a woman got out. She followed the stepping
stones through the gravel, went up the porch steps, and disappeared into the house through the front door as the shouts of
small children reached our ears.

"We can knock," Yongwon suggested.

I smiled and shook my head. "I wouldn't know what to say."

So we turned and walked further up the hill instead, hand
in hand. And I was ready—"for as it turns out," in the words of
Amor Towles, "one can visit the past quite pleasantly, as long as

one does so expecting nearly every aspect of it to have changed."[1] We passed a house I did not recognize and a pristine paved street that wound away to the right through the former cow pasture, and then we halted on the crest. The meadow was still there.

It was still there, and the new route for Highway 421 now divided it into two unequal pieces. The bright autumn sunshine glinted off pebble-sized cars as they whisked along and disappeared around the curve of a hill.

But though I felt a bit heartsore to see that prosaic yellow median and black asphalt in the distance, I knew for certain then that I had not come to pay homage to that place as a shrine. I greeted it as an old friend instead—one on whom the years had left their mark, as they had on me—and took a handful of photos without trying to take it all in, so that I could pore over the main features later.

One last glance, and we headed back to the car.

When I look at the images now, I see that the trees in the gap have grown tall. The light is the way I remember it, scattering into soft hues of green and gold and brown between the lengthening autumn shadows of branching crowns. Beauty still dwells there.

I think of a comment C. S. Lewis made to a resident who lived only two hours away from this region: "The new photos raise extreme *Sehnsucht*: each a landscape as fulfils [sic] my dreams. *That* is the America I wd. [sic] like to see, not the great cities, which, except superficially, are really much the same all over the earth."[2] Earlier, to the same correspondent, he wrote that

1. Amor Towles, *A Gentleman in Moscow* (New York: Viking, 2016), 461.

2. Lewis to Mary Van Deusen, June 6, 1952, *The Collected Letters of C. S. Lewis, Vol. III: Narnia, Cambridge and Joy, 1950–1963* (New York: HarperCollins, 2007), 199.

"the landscape lures one into it. I long to be tramping over those wooded—or, what is better, half wooded hills. I'm as sensitive as a German to the spell of *das Ferne* ['the Far country'] and all that."[3] As am I, it seems.

After Lewis's many years of following the ephemeral trail of joy, such moments and sights revealed themselves to be foreshadowings of a greater destination. He wrote about the change this knowledge brought to his view of "the old stab, the old bittersweet," saying,

> When we are lost in the woods the sight of a signpost is a great matter. He who first sees it cries, "Look!" The whole party gathers round and stares. But when we have found the road and are passing signposts every few miles, we shall not stop and stare. They will encourage us and we shall be grateful to the authority that set them up. But we shall not stop and stare, or not much; not on this road, though their pillars are of silver and their lettering of gold. "We would be at Jerusalem."[4]

At my desk, I trace the contours of the meadow like the weathered crevices of an old beam. I understand that I was never meant to linger here. At the same time, I am grateful for this signpost. This one and all the rest are more precious to me now

---

3. Lewis to Mary Van Deusen, May 5, 1952, *The Collected Letters of C. S. Lewis, Vol. III*, 186.

4. C. S. Lewis, *Surprised by Joy: The Shape of My Early Life* (San Diego: Harcourt Brace, 1955), 238.

that I know what they mean; now that I believe Christ has gone to prepare a place for me, I am free to receive the signposts as aids intentionally sent. For the journey of this rich, humorous, grace-pierced faith has never been merely a question of cerebral comprehension and assent; it is an odyssey Home to—and *with*—a God who has asked everything of me: heart, soul, mind, strength. In the face of my own tendencies to wander or linger along the way, the sweetly barbed longing is just deep and frequent enough to keep me tender—and moving.

I let out a soft laugh, suddenly overcome by a sense of deep grace. He saw the small girl in whose heart the stirrings for Home would begin kindling in earnest on this hilltop. I think over the many signposts I have passed, beginning with this earliest that still shines in my memory, and I see now the gift that the Father of lights has left here for me.

Although so many of the landmarks from my childhood and adolescence have passed away and been razed to the ground, he allowed the meadow to remain.

And he put a road right through it.

PART

2

*Living
Homeward*

I, a pilgrim of eternity, stand before Thee, O eternal One.
Let me not seek to deaden or destroy the desire for Thee
that disturbs my heart. Let me rather yield myself to its
constraint and go where it leads me. Make me wise to see
all things to-day under the form of eternity, and make me
brave to face all the changes in my life which such a vision
may entail: through the grace of Christ my Saviour. Amen.

John Baillie, *A Diary of Private Prayer*, Twelfth Day: Morning

6

As an Exile

Sometime in the tenth century, an Old English poem is recorded in a work that will come to be known as the Exeter Book. It is a poem about an unmoored exile who has lost his home and now roves the earth searching for a new one.

The main speaker of "The Wanderer" staggers between two realities: memories of feasting in mead halls with his late beloved lord, and his present sorrow among "yellow waves" where frost and snow fall, mingled with hail.

The world is ever only on loan, he reflects, and its glory passes away: "So this middle-earth each day fails and falls. . . . Here wealth is fleeting, here friend is fleeting, here man is fleeting, here woman is fleeting—all this earthly habitation shall be emptied."[1] The thoughts are raw, the anguish ragged.

---

1. "The Wanderer," trans. E. T. Donaldson, in *The Norton Anthology of English Literature*, 7th ed., Vol. 1., eds. M. H. Abrams et al. (New York: W. W. Norton, 2000), 101–2.

But it is the poet who wraps up the soliloquy of the earth-walker and has the last word:

> Wel bið þam þe him are seceð,
> frofre to Fæder on heofonum,
> þær us eal seo fæstnung stondeð.[2]

> It will be well with him who seeks favor,
> comfort from the Father in heaven,
> where for us all stability resides.[3]

A thousand years later, scholars and critics will respond to this closing with ambivalence. Here is a "characteristic Old English injunction to practice restraint on earth, place hope only in heaven," according to one introduction.[4] Some wonder if "The Wanderer" was written by a pagan poet and "reworked" by a Christian,[5] and some who call the context "unequivocally Christian" still draw a distinction between the "secular lament" of the wanderer himself and the Christian consolation of the end.[6] Others find the contrast jarring: "[The wanderer] laments his own loss and the inevitability of loss with a poignancy that is not balanced by the brief introduction and conclusion in the voice of a Christian moralist."[7]

---

2. "The Wanderer," n.d.

3. "The Wanderer," trans. Donaldson, 102. Line breaks have been added.

4. Introduction to "The Wanderer" in *The Norton Anthology of English Literature*, 100.

5. Kevin Crossley-Holland, ed. *The Anglo-Saxon World: An Anthology* (New York: Oxford University Press, 2009), 47.

6. Richard Marsden, ed. *The Cambridge Old English Reader*, 2nd ed. (Cambridge: Cambridge University Press, 2015), 342.

7. Peter S. Baker, *Introduction to Old English*, 2nd ed. (Malden, MA: Blackwell, 2007), 234.

The ending is out of joint with the rest of the text, they suggest. What are we to make of it? In the face of the poem's sorrows, how can this terse conclusion ring true?

◇ ◇ ◇

I am homesick, I think.

It is August 1995, and my view from the ninth floor of an apartment building in Seoul looks nothing like the muted blue and green Appalachian Mountains of my childhood. Concrete villas and low brick buildings sprawl out below me, crowned with bright yellow water tanks and electric red crosses. Mountains blur the left edge of the veranda glass like a stray eyelash in the corner of my sight, but these seem darker and more imposing than the ones I have known.

I look, and I weep, for all the miles between me and the places that have brought me happiness. For that final, strangely poignant moment in North Carolina when we left the playground for the last time, and I knew I could never come to it as a child again— and perhaps, after time and development had gnawed through the land, never see it again at all.

I wrap my arms around my knees. My aunt crouches close and pats my back. "Don't cry," she says. "Don't cry; you'll make your parents sad."

I do my best to stanch my tears, but the sadness stems from more than a change of location. Months before arriving in Korea, I witnessed a suicide threat. The image of the incident is branded into my memory and my outlook on the world, and I now carry a suffocating fear with me: a belief that it is my responsibility to keep my friends and family—everyone I love—alive, and happy enough to want to stay alive. I do not confide this fear to anyone, but in it I feel a cold, matter-of-fact severance from my childhood. Nothing is familiar. Lives are terribly, terribly fragile. I wish I could trace my path just a few steps backward, but what separates me from my old home cannot be bridged.

This sense of helplessness, weeks later, prods me to listen carefully to my homeroom teacher's explanation of Christ. At eleven I relinquish my life to the Lord I've sought, one way or another, all my life. I try to settle into the language and the story that has caught me up and seems to be carrying me along. Now I know where I am truly bound; now, surely, all my unsettledness will be laid to rest. The ache will cease.

But it doesn't.

Something akin to it ambushes me in high school, in a whirlwind of crisping leaves that sweeps around my shoulders and knees on a gray afternoon.

Again, in college, in a stream of color cascading from the stained glass windows of the university chapel.

At first I think it must be homesickness once more, hitting like a fresh blow somewhere over my heart. But there is a sweeter quality to this than the mingling of fear and grief that my aunt saw; it is tinged with the surrender of a laugh that comes after a long cry. Encountering it is like gulping a tonic that makes me thirstier the more I drink, and as irrational as it seems, I want more of this "inconsolable longing,"[8] as C. S. Lewis would call it. *Why?* I wonder. *What am I missing?*

---

8. C. S. Lewis, *Surprised by Joy: The Shape of My Early Life* (San Diego: Harcourt Brace, 1955), 72.

How can this ache be so strong still?

◇ ◇ ◇

Years later, as I skim an old textbook from college, a literary motif teaches me to delve deeper.

Ubi sunt is a Latin phrase meaning "where are [they]?" and it appears as a line of questioning that became popular in medieval works after the Roman philosopher Boethius used it in *The Consolation of Philosophy.* "The Wanderer" echoes with it in an elegiac Anglo-Saxon context:

> Where has the horse gone? Where the young
>   warrior?
> Where is the giver of treasure? What has become
>   of the feasting seats?
> Where are the joys of the hall?
> Alas, the bright cup! Alas, the mailed warrior!
>   Alas, the prince's glory!
> How that time has gone, vanished beneath
>   night's cover, just as if it had never been![9]

The questions are rhetorical. The wandering warrior does not expect an answer from any quarter, but he voices his inquiry anyway.

Silence meets his words; it is as if they ricochet everywhere in search of a presence that should be but no longer is. And in them I begin to perceive a pain that lies at the heart of my longing.

---

9. "The Wanderer," trans. Donaldson, 101. Line breaks have been added.

This is loss. In the stark bereavement of the Wanderer's words, I look back across my own past places and relationships and realize that I have lost "home" more profoundly than I have ever known it.

In my life I have missed nooks and vistas that are half a world away, and earlier times when it seems I bore lighter burdens than the ones I carry now. Yet what I truly miss comes from a deeper sundering; I am missing the wholeness of a world that I have only ever experienced in shards.

The Christian faith speaks of grace and redemption at length, but being part of that true story means we recognize the ravages of what we have lost: the loss of Eden, the loss of unhindered communion with God. We see daily the distortion and absence of real love. And the loss is ongoing; as mortals we know the devastation that comes inevitably with the ebb of time—places erased, bodies deteriorating, loved ones gone.

But the acknowledgment of this loss, I am learning, is a vital part of the longing we bear.

What has become of us? Where have our friends and family gone? Where are the trust and the enthusiasm that used to flow so easily from us? What has happened to this relationship—that old favorite spot—these intervening years? *Ubi sunt* is one way to begin the first step of grief.

Asked in the pattern set by the Wanderer, *ubi sunt* questions name what is missing. They give us a sense of the gaps that have opened in our lives and prepare us for the voids in which we will walk as we mourn.

But there is a wondering underneath such questions as well. When we ask, "Where are they?" and "Where is the goodness that used to be?" we are also asking, "Which way is up?" "Where am I supposed to be now, when I feel unable to move?" "How are we to go on?"

I have never been comfortable with pouring out my grief in this way, and at times I have been afraid that releasing certain reservoirs of hidden pain will drown me. Yet the lamenters of the Psalms, Christians throughout the ages, and Christ himself on Calvary were willing to voice their questions without an immediate resolution. They knew that to ask them in the presence of God meant something different from letting them dissipate into the air. Their willingness, their courage to be so vulnerable before the Father, opens a way for us to acknowledge the absences we feel.

Ultimately, to gloss over the losses sustained in the fall of man and its reverberations would be to deny the cost of the rescue, the worth of our ransom, and the surpassing joy Christ saw that made him scorn the shame of the cross (Heb. 12:2 NIV). And it would cause us to miss entirely what is coming.

For the pattern given over and over in Scripture, from God's dealings with Job to Jesus's promise to give his followers a hundredfold what they have left, is of gain outstripping loss. Only as I plumb the agony of separation can I fathom the magnitude of what lies ahead; only as I heft the weight of this day's pain do I know how to fix my eyes on Christ and anticipate the deathless, tearless, painless glory of an eternal tomorrow.

Grief and heartache and wrenching honesty have their place in the Christian life. If we open ourselves up to tears that scald our faces and carve aching hollows in the bottoms of our hearts, we do so in faith that God truly will wipe every tear from our eyes.

In this way, "The Wanderer" reminds me of the freedom we have to weep outright. To spread our empty hands so that we can take up what is to come. "[A] man must never utter too quickly his breast's passion, unless he knows first how to achieve remedy, as a leader with his courage," says the poet. "It will be well with him who seeks favor, comfort from the Father in heaven, where for us all stability resides."[10]

The Wanderer cannot see over the cresting waves or guess how many seas he will have to cross before he finds rest in the hall of his fathers, but he knows where his remedy lies. This is what it is to grieve with hope, as Paul desires for the Thessalonians (1 Thess. 4:13–14). The last line fits because God *is*.

◇ ◇ ◇

I understand, then, that I am Homesick indeed, and that the longing is chronic. I walk about—and write—like a woman with an open wound and a dressing that never seems to stay. This thing gets everlastingly in the way of my living and yet fuels its very core.

But I will find my way home to my liege lord, and on the way I'm discovering that many of us are tucking our chins in against the howling wind and walking on. And as we travel, it's the light from our Home across the sea—the light from his very Person, both before us and within us—that spills out and around our greatest miseries and our dearest hopes, illuminating the losses we carry, and burnishing them with the promise of restoration.

---

10. "The Wanderer," trans. Donaldson, 102.

7

Through the Window of the Imagination

The reach of the sun stooping through the window signals that it is late afternoon and time for a break. I blink out of half sleep; the inked leaves of my notebook arch with a crackle as I lift my hand. My dutifully marked copies of *The Federalist Papers* and *The Tempest* retire to the book pile, and I tug *Prince Caspian* out from underneath.

I turn its pages in my cloistered corner at this university library, beside a high window that frames a view of neo-Gothic limestone buildings and minuscule college students sauntering to unknown destinations. I like the privacy. Hidden in these library stacks, a high school senior can read a children's book without feeling sheepish; here no one sees, no one cares, and no one knows me well enough to raise doubtful eyebrows.

To be honest, no one would look twice even if I were downstairs in the common area. This year in Blacksburg feels like a temporary existence, bookended by our move from Korea in the summer and college looming ahead. Every new tie of friendship

I've made is loosely knotted, every familiar spot tinged with a visitor's detachment. Thus it is odd to me that I've chosen to venture into yet another world—one that isn't even real.

As a child I picked up the Narnia books once, ignorant of their connection to Christ, and skimmed them eagerly for the story. This time, with my attention sharpened by solitude, I can hardly believe this is the same country I visited before. Beckoned by trees and dryads, disappearing islands and singing stars that wake the dawn, my imagination emerges from hiding.

I glance back at a slumbering company as Lucy slips into a moonlit wood. Will the others believe what she sees? Alert and hushed, I watch the little girl draw courage from a great lion's presence. As chapters unfold over days and weeks, I wipe away tears unseen by other humans while a few talking mice move the heart of their Maker to compassion; I laugh quietly at a Marshwiggle's tragic attempts to be cheerful. And when the last king of Narnia hesitates to turn around, suspecting that in a split second he will behold what he has longed all his life to see, my face grows warm with the flash of a kindred hope, and I begin counting the pages left in the seventh book like a traveler guarding her last dwindling handful of coins.

The day the story ends for me, I close *The Last Battle* and sit unmoving in the light. Dust motes flicker over the study carrel. A sort of soul-paralysis takes hold, as if I've lingered too long in another realm and have not been able to get all of myself back to my own world.

It's Aslan, you see, I want to say aloud to someone. All of Narnia has fleshed out truths I know from the Bible; it has lent them humor and texture, creaturely movements and facial expressions.

But in Aslan I see most clearly how careful I've been to keep my imagination under lock and key. I've been reluctant to consider Christ as a real human—so afraid of being presumptuous that I haven't stopped to think about the one-dimensional savior I picture instead.

In my mind, his parables, prayers, and healings are all delivered in the same grave voice and manner. Lewis's Lion, on the other hand, brings together traits I have never thought to think of God: he is wild but good; he can roar to rock the foundations of the earth but also romp like a kitten at play. He sings. He *rejoices*. I have a renewed awe and a compelling desire to draw closer, to inch my way toward him through whatever avenues exist.

I carry a passage by George Müeller with me in an old journal as a guide for how to hear the voice of God. "I seek at the beginning to get my heart into such a state that it has no will of its own in regard to a given matter," Müeller explains. Next, he proceeds to seek the will of God through the Holy Spirit and the Word, taking the circumstances around him into account as well. "Thus, through prayer to God, the study of His Word, and reflection," Müeller makes his decision and moves on.[1] The same journal holds Amy Carmichael's affirmation of the same practice.[2] These words have steadied me through a tumultuous year, and I

---

1. Henry Blackaby, Richard Blackaby, and Claude King, *Experiencing God: Knowing and Doing the Will of God*, rev. ed. (Nashville: B&H, 2008), 115–16.

2. "The devil sometimes speaks and tries to deceive us into thinking it is the voice of God. He tries to get us, who long to walk in the light, to follow instead a will-o-wisp into the marsh. In the matter of guidance there are three important points: 1. The Word of the Lord in the Bible, 2. The Word of the Spirit in our heart, 3. The circumstances of our lives, which have been arranged by God. All three must point one way. It is never enough for any two of them to be taken as showing God's will. *If the voice is God's all three*

am grateful for the direction given by these Christians whose lives in England and India abounded with storied answers to prayer.

But an old wish now stirs again, back from the days when I first learned to pray. What would it be like to see his face while speaking with him, the way the first twelve disciples saw him? How well do I know the voice of my Shepherd apart from seeking it for decision-making? How can his presence become as clear to me as the nearness of Aslan to the Pevensies?

Where is the wood where I may go to find him?

◇ ◇ ◇

In my world, though a passerby would never know it from the still life of assigned books and coffee cups in the library cubicle, all is not well.

Only a few weeks into the school year, my morning street law class began with the usual bell. The teacher was unusually late. My classmates and I shifted in our chairs, lobbing quips and jokes across the aisles, hoping we might have a free period. But soon familiar footsteps sounded in the hallway, and the adventurous ones wilted back into their seats.

Our teacher appeared. "A plane—the news—New York," she said; if there were connecting words, I never caught them. The class was to follow her to the library.

We got up, gathered our things, and cast uncertain looks at one another, wondering if this was some kind of outlandish scenario for which we would need to study precedents and devise

---

will agree" (Elisabeth Elliot, *A Chance to Die: The Life and Legacy of Amy Carmichael* [Grand Rapids: Revell, 1987], 350–51).

prosecution and defense strategies. That was why we were heading to the school library, yes?

But in the library we were motioned to sit at round tables while the teacher wheeled in an old TV on a cart. For the next hour we stared, helpless, at the footage of black clouds pouring from the World Trade Center and of stunned news anchors trying to piece information together on air. Every now and then we glanced searchingly across the tables at one another's faces, but there was no waking from the surreal atmosphere.

A tenth grader got up to pace blindly toward the bookshelves, then back again; in the background was the shrill sound of a woman's voice as she recorded the impact of the second airplane into the second tower. A third report from the Pentagon crowded the screen next. All day, students and teachers moved from classroom to classroom, watching the news, relaying questions without answers, waiting for the next unthinkable event to happen.

Since that day, the gradual flow back to "normalcy" has been jarring. The unrelenting march of the semester has taken me from that library and deposited me in this one, where I have stumbled upon the Narnia series for a second time. I'm not sure I can provide a good reason for reading it; I feel almost guilty for immersing myself in fiction when the world I live in has been so harshly rocked.

If pressed, I'd open the pages of these Chronicles and say that here, too, is a world gone mad. It knows its share of disaster and danger. Yet within its borders I also see celebration and tenacity and resolve; it has given me the possibility of order within chaos, an idea of how to move forward. There is a practical defense to this jaunt into fantasy in 2001, I would say, clumsily; I have simply escaped long enough from my own world to glean useful lessons and return, trading Aslan in for Jesus. A brief whimsical detour for reality.

◊ ◊ ◊

But now a strange and forlorn unsettledness rests on me.

I make guesses in my journal as to its cause, feeling foolish in the process; maybe it's the sheer liveliness of the characters I miss, or the seas and fords and mountain ranges that make up a richer landscape "over there." "Nobility of character," I scribble, guessing. Trust. A code of honor I can understand. In the end, the sentence that best sums up my reaction is so simple and guileless it could have come from a much younger hand: "How I wish Narnia were real."

I try to linger there. In my spare moments, I revisit scenes in the books; I write excerpts beside the Scripture passages they bring to mind; I read *C. S. Lewis' Letters to Children*. In the years that follow, I will repeat this pattern with other works I love; I will plunge into research—biographies, supplementary DVD material, historical context—to see if I can sidle closer to the thing that has drawn me in.

But every time, I will fail.

No matter how fascinating the additional information is, it is never enough; it adds to my knowledge, but not to my joy. The sense of standing on the brink of something beautiful and expansive always fades, no matter how earnestly I try to bottle it or recreate it. I come back to the routines of my own life and still feel the halt of an experience I cannot tame.

One day in college, months after the ache surfaces in my journal, I walk into a bookstore and weave between the display tables. "Explore the World of Narnia," a sign says. From the stacks underneath I pick up a book of summary and criticism. When I place it back on the table two minutes later, the room is cold. The analysis is objective and succinct, as any study guide might be, and it is devoid of the warmth and courage and hope I have been pursuing.

This is my wake-up call.

"A bird on the dissection table," Clyde Kilby contends, "is not a bird. It is a 'specimen.'" The difference between the two involves far more than a beating heart:

> In the laboratory it loses its bird character of fly-
> ing, singing, joyfulness, undulation, rhythm, and
> even its shape. We can learn valuable things by
> dissection, but there is the deception of suppos-
> ing that the dissection will tell us the ultimate
> truth about the bird. It is only in its God-given
> "birdness" that we shall have its high truth.[3]

While Kilby draws the distinction in an essay about beauty in Scripture, this is the very difference I sense while trying to keep my encounter of Narnia "alive." What I desire most is entrance into the *life* of the other world, not a travel brochure memorial-izing what I've glimpsed. Some "high truth" at the center of the story has caught my attention, and I am finding I cannot preserve,

---

3. Clyde S. Kilby, *The Arts and the Christian Imagination: Essays on Art, Literature, and Aesthetics*, eds. William Dyrness and Keith Call (Brewster, MA: Paraclete, 2016), 166–67.

control, or manufacture it any more than a toddler scribbling drawings on endpapers can add to a story's meaning.

I'm tempted to believe, therefore, that I have only two options in the face of this Narnian yearning: to make the impression last as long as it will go, or spurn it altogether and wait for the impact to pass. Why draw it out?

But Kilby drops the hint of a third possibility in his contrast, one that I only begin to understand as I enter adulthood. What if there is a "God-given 'birdness'" to this book-based spark of longing? If it is not a spark that can be preserved or generated by me, can it be meant for some purpose by Another?

Scottish author George MacDonald would say so. He called the "wise imagination" an essential guide in the life of faith,

> for it is not the things we see the most clearly that influence us the most powerfully; undefined, yet vivid visions of something beyond, something which eye has not seen nor ear heard, have far more influence than any logical sequences whereby the same things may be demonstrated to the intellect. . . . We live by faith, and not by sight."[4]

The imagination, in his view, is a faculty enabling humans to see that the "outward world is but a passing vision of the persistent true."[5] And that "persistent true," that "something beyond," is no custom-made fancy.

---

4. George MacDonald, "The Imagination: Its Functions and Its Culture," in *A Dish of Orts* (London: Sampson Low, Marston, 1893).

5. MacDonald, "The Imagination: Its Functions and Its Culture."

In Romans 8, the apostle Paul gives specific detail to this unseen reality, writing that "we hope for what we do not see" (v. 25): freedom from creation's "bondage to corruption," a glad fulfillment of its "pains of childbirth," and "the glory that is to be revealed to us" (vv. 18–24). All these elements are part of the splendor Lewis's books held out to me in high school; they were the truth that gave the setting its vitality. I thought I was retreating into a children's book series in secret, but all the while—as Paul puts it—the "eyes of [my] heart" were being opened to "what is the hope of his calling, what is the wealth of his glorious inheritance in the saints, and what is the immeasurable greatness of his power toward us who believe, according to the mighty working of his strength" (Eph. 1:18–19 csb). My sight was never the same again.

For we do live in two worlds. The kingdom of God has yet to be revealed in fullness (Luke 19:11), but it is also here in our midst already (Matt. 12:28; Luke 17:21). Its denizens are called to the real work of feeding the hungry and welcoming strangers, but they must also engage in the real work of wrestling not "against flesh and blood, but against the rulers, against the authorities, against the cosmic powers over this present darkness, against the spiritual forces of evil in the heavenly places" (Eph. 6:12). Present and future, seen and unseen.

Ultimately, Narnia opened my eyes to the immediate presence of another reality alongside my tangible one—and the call I have as a human being to engage in both. It is in *this* world, with its breaking news reports and quotidian library corners, that "we have battle and blazing eyes, / And chance and honour and high surprise."[6] To this world the only Son of a divine Sovereign came—and died, came to life again, and rose up into the sky until a cloud hid him—telling his followers that he was going ahead to prepare a Home where he would dwell with them (John 14:2–3). In my own corner of this earth, a doorway between the visible and invisible now stands permanently open for me to come before the throne of grace (Heb. 4:16). It seems I do not need midnight access to an enchanted forest so much as I need eyes to see the strange wonder of the tale I am already in.

The flashes of my captivated imagination reveal a reality that already exists. Knowing this, I am freed from both the sorrow of watching them fade and the need to deaden my response to their occurrence. I am able to move my limbs after a nourishing read and contemplate hope again because there is an antidote to the sting: the knowledge that the eyes of my heart have not, in these glimpses, played me false. As I step into the high truths of a hidden kingdom, growing younger in trust and wonder as I learn to live by its code, the sparks become a compass, a tuning fork, a bright guide in the dark.

A waking I can welcome.

◇ ◇ ◇

When she is five, she tells me she's been reading a chapter every day.

---

6. G. K. Chesterton, "The House of Christmas," in *Poems* (New York: John Lane, 1916), section IV, accessed March 1, 2023, https://www.gutenberg.org/files/31184/31184-h/31184-h.htm.

Every night I kneel for a little while beside my older daughter's bed to hear about her day, pray with her, and sing two verses of her lullaby hymn. On Fridays I stretch out beside her on the bed frame her daddy made, and we talk.

Tonight the subject is Narnia. She has figured out that an English torch is an American flashlight—"because you can't save the battery on a burning stick!" She spells out the different ways Aslan brings children to Narnia in each book, "like when he opened the back of the wardrobe so Lucy could come through and have tea with Mr. Tumnus, but closed it so the others couldn't see and only she could." She wonders why.

We talk on, about the blitz, and Israelite spies, and Maleficent from *Sleeping Beauty*—"Of shoes—and ships—and sealing-wax— / Of cabbages—and kings"[7]—and then, with the air of one making a careful confession, she says, "I've been searching for secret doors and cupboards in the house to see if there's a way into Narnia." Her eyes suddenly turn toward my face, searching to see if this grown-up will laugh.

Warmed by this forthright confession, the kindred searcher in me rouses from slumber. My daughter must tap and try many doors on her own, and I know I cannot travel her journey for her. But perhaps I can help her set out.

Breaking the hush, I twinkle my eyes at her and return the privilege of her confidence. "I've done that too."

---

7. Lewis Carroll, "The Walrus and the Carpenter," in *Through the Looking-Glass* (London, 1872).

8

In the Company of Other Pilgrims

Heels. Dress shoes. A pair of cowboy boots. The door of the coffee shop swings open and thumps shut, and in between the staccato steps of each customer beat out an irregular rhythm on the wooden floorboards. I listen for them under the sporadic blast of the espresso machine. I breathe in the bitter-smooth smell of coffee and count the number of laptops plugged in along the bar at the window. For my next mental feat, I may try to guess which person will answer to the next name the barista calls. Anything, basically, that will keep me from having to glance across the table at my friend.

We have reached an impasse in our growing reluctance to talk to and spend time with each other. Neither of us knows how the coolness started. She is studying her cuticles as diligently as I am examining my side of the room; we are only at this table because of the undaunted coordination of a mutual friend, who now sits between our set, nonconfrontational jawlines.

I could leave. It would be a simple act to follow a passing pair of shoes to the door, to stretch this taut silence with more distance and sever it cleanly with a closing push of the knob.

But I can't. A sigh of resignation leaks from me as I realize that leaving will only delay this conversation; if I walk away, I will have to sit down at some other table days from now with the same people. Their presence is unavoidable; if I don't run into them at Friday large group, I'll see them at Sunday chapel. But more significantly, I'm already learning that this rift will glare like a chasm at my feet every time I approach God to offer "[my] gift at the altar" (Matt. 5:23–24). And as hard as it is to admit, I've been missing the dimpled, candid spontaneity of my friend.

I swivel in my chair, turning back to the faces that know me. We might as well get to work.

In one way, I'm here because of mounting mutual frustration with a friend. In another, I am here because a campus Bible study leader planted her foot in my dorm room doorway during my first year at college.

After noting my absence of several weeks, through which I had hoped to fade away unnoticed, Michelle came to find me. "Even if you don't come to my small group," she said, "you need to find a community to grow in as a Christian." The grave tone in her ordinarily cheery voice made me take notice. Even so, I might have dismissed her words after she left, but I happened to be reading C. S. Lewis's essay titled "Membership" that week.

"We are forbidden to neglect the assembling of ourselves together," Lewis wrote. "Christianity is already institutional in the earliest of its documents. The Church is the Bride of Christ. We are members of one another."[1] Together he and Michelle drove the point home, and I lowered the shield of my introverted reluctance and took it to heart. Since the organization that hosted the Bible study didn't offer larger gatherings or Sunday services, I looked up other campus fellowships and joined one.

Gradually I was folded into a student group that encompassed a variety of fields. Engineering and English majors, prelaw and premed folk, education and architecture students attended Sunday chapel together and carpooled for late-night meals after Friday-evening meetings. The personalities I met spanned an even wider spectrum: outgoing, assertive, timid, brash, motherly, fastidious, mellow. In spite of these differences, a sense of connection brought the members together into various permutations week by week through study sessions and coffee dates and class potluck dinners.

I still felt tentative and reserved in that new environment, but being among so many made me dare to think that meaningful connections could be made, and I prayed for one or two close friends.

Two years in, I had gained them—and I also noticed I was thawing. After moving out of the first-year dorms, I lived near a cluster of friends who were Christ followers, many of whom attended the same fellowship. Someone was always cooking or baking something, it seemed: stuffed mushrooms for the neighbors, spring rolls with peanut sauce for a shared dinner, ramen noodles for a study break. The ambient sounds of our apartments were composed of light knocks on room doors and the strumming

---

1. C. S. Lewis, "Membership," in *The Weight of Glory: And Other Addresses* (New York: HarperSanFrancisco, 1949), 158.

of guitars, interspersed with serious conversations or moments of hilarity.

Once, at a debriefing meeting for an inner-city ministry team, someone came up with the idea to start a percussive beat with kitchen tools and office supplies. I was handed a pair of scissors to add a wispy click; around the room, cups, spoons, and pens pounded and tapped out an elaborate rhythm. It was altogether exhilarating and ridiculous, but somehow we each kept our parts going even as we dissolved in laughter. In this environment, month after month, many of my defenses and overly careful conversational habits began to melt away.

For the first time, then, I have found myself in a community that operates on the assumption—sometimes explicitly spoken, most often quietly demonstrated—that Christians are family: "one body in Christ, and individually members one of another" (Rom. 12:5). I've met people whose opinions I trust, who generously clear a chair for me when I need a listening ear or an honest rebuke. It is undeniably difficult at times, especially when habits and opinions clash, but an undeniable goodness is soaking into my bones as well. Through the people around me, I am starting to see what it means to be a part of the body of Christ.

Even the conflict that has led me here to this coffee shop is a sign that we two have chosen to let each other matter. After an hour or two of honest rambling, my friend and I discover that while I value lengthy conversations involving ideas and dreams, she prefers activities that allow friends to simply enjoy being together.

"Sometimes I just need you to go shopping or walking or browsing movies with me," she confides, "without, you know . . ."

"Overspiritualizing everything?" I suggest, a rueful grin tugging at the edge of my mouth. Suddenly I glimpse how my earnestness must feel to her—how it must have felt to look for connection and be met with seriousness most of the time.

Thankfully she laughs, and the air clears again.

A few weeks later, I pick her up in front of her apartment. "What shall we do today?"

She shrugs, and then stamps her flip-flops with enthusiasm as an idea strikes. "I know. Let's go for a drive."

As I roll out of the parking lot, she reclines the passenger seat all the way back, tilting her unclouded face to the open window. MercyMe's "I Can Only Imagine" plays into the breeze, and we listen without speaking, basking in the sunlight as it falls through the moonroof, absorbing the words along with the warmth. It is the simplest of spring afternoons, and our contentment as we think about our eternal Home side by side sears into my memory as a beautiful thing.

◇ ◇ ◇

Four o'clock is the stagnant hour of the day.

By this time, I've usually run out of creative steam. My tiny daughter and I have read through all of her board books multiple times, played peekaboo with the baby in the mirror, laughed together over stolen noses and tickly fingertips, filled up the day's quota for tummy time, and finished all the infant stimulation activities I can think of.

The hush of the still house presses against my temples and lungs. But the baby is awake, so I put her in the infant carrier and wander out to the porch. I sway with her, singing hymns into the soft down of her dark hair, and look down the street for Yongwon's car.

The sun, white-hot, hovers over the Front Range. Cliff swallows swoop to and fro, daubing mud nests under the eaves of stucco houses. I finish the fifth verse and start a new hymn, feeling my heart falter, trying not to think of how to make tomorrow feel distinct from today. I crane forward and watch the corner as if Yongwon will appear any moment, though it will be an hour and twenty minutes before he actually arrives.

My husband is the only person I know in this new town. Doors to other relationships, tentatively tried, have closed. Not too long ago, I went on a few walks with the wife of one of Yongwon's coworkers, but these came to an end due to an order forbidding fraternization between government employees and contractors, including family members. Small-group gatherings were already on hold for the summer when we joined our new church. Upon our completion of the membership class, the ministry coordinator gave a meaningful glance at my third-trimester curve and said, "Normally this is where we would plug you into a team, but we really think you should take the time to concentrate on your growing family." Our mentor couple nodded quickly, smiling for us, and sent us home. They meant well, I know, but when my mother left after two months of invaluable help and companionship, I realized there was no one I could ask to hold the baby for a few minutes while I tried to collect my sleep-deprived wits.

Four o'clock. Five o'clock. Six.

A gnawing, sourceless sense of dread begins to dog my steps, first in the evenings, then the mornings. Dutifully I seek out books and Bible studies that talk about the gift of motherhood, nap when the baby naps, and try to treasure the fleeting moments, but eventually I begin to feel like an invalid trying to keep down a relentless tide of stomach sickness. I am fighting not to slip into a pit of disorientation every waking hour, and the struggle devours most of my energy.

Out of nowhere, I think of a dream I once read about in which the dreamer fell off a cliff and kept falling, falling, falling:

> [A]s I fell I kept my eyes open and watched the darkness turn from gray-black to black, from black to jet black and from jet black to a pure liquid blackness which I could touch with my hands but which I could not see. But I went on falling, and it was so black that there was nothing anywhere and it was not any use doing anything or caring or thinking because of the blackness and because of the falling. It was not any use.[2]

I am plummeting. For some reason I must believe it's still worth it to battle the darkness, given the effort I expend in thrashing and curling in as I fall, but there is no bottom.

Somehow I have lost all my reference points. I cannot seem to remember who I am or where I am bound.

◇ ◇ ◇

I glance at the time.

---

2. Roald Dahl, "A Piece of Cake: First Story-1942," in *The Wonderful Story of Henry Sugar and Six More* (New York: Alfred A. Knopf, 1977), 224.

Although I was scheduled for an hour-long session, the counselor has let me talk for two. She's been jotting line after line on her clipboard, and I wonder what her verdict will be.

During a chaotic gathering of parents and toddlers a few days ago, a stray thought flitted through my head so quickly that it startled me: *What if I didn't feel this overwhelmed and full of fear all the time?* An answering wish, almost clipping the heels of the first in its desperate hope, tumbled after it: *I want to be better. I want to be well.*

On the way home, I turned to Yongwon and said, "What would you think if I started taking medication?"

"Medication for what?" he replied.

"For depression." A dam I didn't know existed broke then, and I cried the entire way home as we talked. It was an indescribable relief to point out the leaden shadow that had been dogging my steps and robbing me of my joy for weeks. But I also hesitated. A novice at understanding mental health, I felt somehow that I should have been able to throw off this weight through some kind of spiritual discipline. Tentatively I asked Yongwon if he thought taking medication would signal a failure of faith on my part.

He was silent for a second. "If I have a headache and need to take a pill, that doesn't mean I have too little faith. If I break my arm and go to the emergency room, that doesn't mean I've had too little faith. So, no." His words called back a passage by Mary Beth Chapman that I had recently read:

> The Prozac was not an instant fix-it kind of drug. It was medication, like high blood pressure medication. It treated my symptoms. As I started feeling better, I could then work on the root of

the problem and begin to heal from things in the
past. It helped me clearly think about how God's
grace applied to me.[3]

The crushing load lifted a little from my shoulders, and I sagged
at the sudden release. At home I gathered up what shreds of courage remained to me and called a list of counselors, making an
appointment in the end with this one.

At long last, the counselor looks up and surprises me. "In this
particular case, I don't think you need medication. Sometimes we
do. Right now, I think you need *people*." I look at her wonder-
ingly. "How about a little homework? When you come back, tell
me what your week would look like if you were back in Virginia."

It is startling how much insight a well-timed question can
yield. Before I leave the building, my mind starts to fill out the
answer in swift brushstrokes. If we were back in Virginia, our
undergraduate friends would be coming by to see the baby; her
small milestones would be magnified by their fascination, on top
of my own. I know the favorite lunch spots where I could venture
out to get a quick bite between feedings and the patches of lawn
scattered about town where we would teach her to run barefoot.

The counselor's question is the first of many small events that
feel like stepping stones dotting the way out of a quagmire. After
I ask for prayer at our multigenerational small group, another
mother—in her second trimester herself—kindly offers to babysit
our little one. On social media I come across the video of a friend's
child learning to navigate the stairs, which helps me imagine our

---

3. Mary Beth Chapman, with Ellen Vaughn, *Choosing to See: A Journey of
Struggle and Hope* (Grand Rapids: Revell, 2010), 70.

daughter doing the same someday. I start a daily schedule and the vital practice of putting "things to look forward to" on our calendar, beginning with a short road trip to visit friends in Wyoming. Though I have always thought of myself as an introvert, I can't help but notice that all these life-giving items are coming through other humans.

My steps are hesitant and tottering; each day I wonder if the ground of my stabilizing thoughts will hold, or if it will give way and plunge me back into darkness. But the cooling air seems easier to inhale as autumn comes, and though I do not dare to note it out loud at first, it carries the impossible but unmistakable azure crispness of new hope.

◇ ◇ ◇

Friendships, of course, do not spring up magically out of the ground overnight. The college fellowship setting was as concentrated as a greenhouse, with all its growth burgeoning under a common shelter and flourishing in double time as we breathed the same air and lived in close proximity to one another. Out in the wider expanse of Colorado and new motherhood, as I'm discovering, the conditions are different. Opportunities to meet are less frequent and interruptions legion; getting to know people simply takes longer. Here, the language of affection seems to be expressed through occasional phone texts and playdates and meal trains in times of crises, and I am learning how to combine it with the dialects of care I know.

On a summer morning I bake blueberry muffins and tiptoe across the street, leaving them at the front door of a friendly neighbor whose infant is in the NICU. Every step, even a smile across the circle to another mother at the library's toddler story time, takes time and initiative, but small, kind responses lend me strength enough to keep moving forward.

Maybe this might be a good time, once again, to ask my Father for friends and mentors. For people.

The embodied answers come a little at a time. We join a smaller church. By the time I go into labor with our second daughter in the middle of an autumn night, we have a short list of friends we can call, and one of them arrives in our living room in fifteen minutes. Another friend takes the time to cook and bring us a pot of savory Korean *miyeokguk* for my recovery—a gesture that makes my eyes brim for months. Their readiness to love in tangible ways expands my own, teaching me to ask myself in future situations if I can do a little bit more for someone else.

Two years later, I venture out to attend a choral sing with a friend. I stay behind to help put the chairs away and strike up a conversation with a couple who want to bring about a renaissance of the Christian imagination; their openness and enthusiasm lead to my involvement with the Anselm Society and eventually the staff of its arts guild. Similar trails lead out from other encounters: from a friendship that starts in our Bible study, our family leaves our small church with a blessing to join an even smaller church plant; from a few discussions about educational options for our children, I find two dear women who become like sisters. Tiny, almost happenstance beginnings grow to a magnitude that floors me, and at times I am overwhelmed to think what God must have known was in store when he brought us here so many years ago.

In general, these friendships start with the exchange of thoughts on common interests. A spark of resonance grows into a mutual flame of understanding. The attitude or stance of the other person matters—the way they express themselves, and not merely what they say. Somewhere along the way, vulnerability enters in: one person takes the risk of sharing a burden or is forced to share a need, and the other responds. And so the bond grows. One milestone I find especially meaningful is the moment when one person goes out of his or her way to say an impulsive "I love you" or "I'm thankful to have you in my life" to another. And I notice that in every close relationship, at least for me, there is a point at which you decide to throw your lot in with the other person—a point beyond which their suffering means your suffering, and their good news, your genuine relief and deep celebration.

Some of the best times of fellowship I know come within these relationships, calling back earlier moments like the car ride in college. If someone had asked me then what fellow believers had to do with the Homeward ache, I would probably have said that such community is good for "[stirring] up one another to love and good works, not neglecting to meet together, . . . encouraging one another, and all the more as [we] see the Day drawing near" (Heb. 10:24–25). It is incomparably sweet to spend time with someone else who shares the longing for that Day.

Yet while such moments are gifts, increasingly I find that it isn't those shared minutes of contemplation that spread the goodness of the new creation before me.

It's the people themselves.

It's the friend from the coffee shop conversation who went on to harness her improvisational creativity, creating an art show based on the color white that included an exquisite pair of wings made of interlacing cotton swabs. It's the husband whose solid presence helped me take my recovery step-by-step, who now approaches woodworking with the same patience and respect for the physicality of God's creation. It is the artists I am privileged to know—the musicians, the poets, the potters, the world builders—who take their hands away from their hearts to hold out their work to others, though it will leave them vulnerable.

I watch those around me settle into who they are, and sometimes they act in curious ways, no matter where their work space is, as if they are out to spend their lives. A doctor finds out that a very ill patient has no appetite for anything besides chocolate cake, so he brings a homemade one to the patient's next appointment. Two foster parents pray for each therapist they work with, seeking to honor the individuals involved in the stories of the children in their care. A mother training to become an Anglican deacon serves the people in her parish with extraordinary thoughtfulness, while her husband makes nourishing art out of everything he puts his hand to, whether in a bakery or in their kitchen.

Living among other humans gives me an idea of the complex—though consistent—personhood of God. According to Herman Bavinck, a Dutch Reformed theologian, "the image of God is much too rich for it to be fully realized in a single human being, however richly gifted that human being may be. It can only be somewhat unfolded in its depth and riches in a humanity counting billions of members."[4] Even within the small sampling I know out of those billions of members, I am discovering trait after

---

4. Herman Bavinck, *In the Beginning: Foundations of Creation Theology*, ed. John Bolt, trans. John Vriend (Grand Rapids: Baker, 1999), 212.

trait of the Father in the children who take after him, and who together "are all part of [the] building in which God himself lives by his spirit" (Eph. 2:22 PHILLIPS). On my clearest days I see how he is fitting us together; I see how he designed the Homeward road to be one we cannot walk alone.

When we are finally gathered Home, we will fill a house with many rooms, Christ says (John 14:1–4). I don't know exactly what this will look like, but I imagine the warmth of a city where people can run upstairs and pop in at an open door to offer another a bite of a fresh concoction or the newly penned verse of a song. I think of what it might be like to sit down at a table across from a person I knew in the old earth and hear about what befell them in the intervening time.

And then I try to contemplate what it will be like in that Day when they are healed of all trauma and hurt, when they no longer have to do the remedial or maintenance work of mortals, and when—free of relational scars, threats of harm, and every kind of burden—they are able to take up all their skill and passion and enthusiasm and artistry in the full work of delighting in their Creator and the world he has restored. But I don't get very far. The thoughts turn to questions as my imagination shorts out.

What will it be like to live among people who love God wholeheartedly, who have learned to look to the interests of others and now have unlimited supplies and empathy and time at their disposal to continue in these things? What will they do, these "members of one another," when they have not thirty or forty years, but eternity?

How will we dwell among such beauty and not be blinded by awe all our days?

9

With Temporary Homes

Early on a Sunday morning in Kentucky, a fictional barber walks through the woods and finds an overlook at the base of a tree. He sits in the spring warmth for a long time; he sits to remember, letting memories from his past come coursing of their own accord.

The memories bend and flow between the house of his childhood down below and the byways he once made in the name of exploration and errands. To this house and the fabric of its life he was brought after the deaths of his parents, and from them he was taken away after the death of his great-aunt. Now, some thirteen years later, he has returned.

When he recounts this moment from the vantage point of seventy-two years, Jayber Crow notes the change that came to him as a young man embracing his roots: "I began to live in my losses," he writes. "Nothing would ever be simple for me again. I never again would be able to put my life in a box and carry it away."[1] His life gained a known-ness and a rhythm among the people who remembered him, including the ones who had long since passed away: "In my comings and goings I crossed their tracks, and my own earlier ones, many times a day, weaving an invisible web that was as real as the ground it was woven over, and as I went about I would feel my losses and my debts."[2]

From the hillside, his mind follows the radial threads of that web. He traces the movements of those who came before him as the nearby river swells in song.

After he rises, the barber walks to the home where he was born and finally arrives in the graveyard, where the men and women whose lives carved a way for his now rest. His later pen spells out the gravity of heart that meets him there:

> The grief that came to me then was nothing like the grief I had felt for myself alone. . . . This grief had something in it of generosity, some nearness to joy. In a strange way it added to me what I had lost. I saw that, for me, this country would always be populated with presences and absences, presences of absences, the living and the dead. The world as it is would always be a reminder of the world that was, and of the world that is to come.[3]

---

1. Wendell Berry, *Jayber Crow* (Berkeley: Counterpoint, 2000), 130.
2. Berry, *Jayber Crow*, 130–31.
3. Berry, *Jayber Crow*, 132.

Jayber's walk moves to the tempo of a hallowed patience, which rolls through his words as clearly as ripples of circadian light coming and going upon the surface of the water.

Something in this cadence stirs up a memory for me. In North Carolina, a little girl puts out her hand and brushes it back and forth in the same measured rhythm over the tops of bluets and buttercups by a creek.

I have ridden my bicycle down the hill from our home to wander a little while before dinner. I'm in no danger of getting lost; I've lived in condominium complexes on both the lower and upper ends of this valley, and I know where every daring tuft of grass has forayed onto the road between the two points.

The hills on either side rise like the walls of a gallery. There, off in the distance, is a crumbling brown barn that sometimes appears in my dreams. Here is the spot where we parked the car the night our unit nearly flooded. My father carried me on his back through knee-high water; I huddled under blankets in the back seat while my mother scooped water off the floor of the car with a plastic bowl and flung it out the window. Over in the next parking lot, Amie's dad once killed a copperhead—a convincing reason to stay away from the shadows under the stilted porches.

I am pedaling uphill now, the incline steep enough for my short height that I have to stand up off my seat the entire way. My nose wrinkles as I pass another frog, the second this week, ironed out flat like a soda can by an unconcerned driver. I swoop around a corner, tilting madly to the side, and wish the boy who once lived a few houses down could be here to see it; he and I made an art form out of angling as low as possible on our turns without scraping ourselves on the ground. Robert has moved away, though. We granted him a double turn in kickball at school on his last day, as a parting gift.

I wheel the bike up the sidewalk, passing Iris's condo. Her mountain laurels are in full glory this summer: fragrant, miniature open umbrellas. But I know better than to put my fingertips in their enticingly perfect but stubbornly sticky cups; I learned that lesson last week. Right before I run up the wooden steps and open my front door, I turn to look out over the parking lot. Tomorrow I'll follow the avenue down through the trees again.

At eight, I know the goodness of a life shaped by a location.

But in a few years and for a long time afterward, I cease to know places where I can walk so confidently, ankle-deep in small landmarks whose lore I know. My mental map is gradually taken up more by blank spaces than the crowding of dots. The losses I witness are scattered throughout one country and then another like feathers, the evidence of their existence blowing away over time. Absences surface not through physical reminders but through intentional reminiscences, photographs, and videos—and often in snapshots I am unaware my mind is taking until I crane backward in thought. I pass from North Carolina to Korea to Virginia to Colorado Springs, moving through each place for a season, never expecting to remain.

Until, in 2012, my husband comes to sit beside me in the living room and puts his hand palm up. I reach over and clasp it.

We are silent in the press of a problem we do not wholly understand. Yongwon's work environment has grown adversarial and strained over the past few months. The more we've prayed, the worse the situation has become. I watch his face in the mornings as I wave goodbye along with our toddler; the days are exacting their toll, leaving him drawn and gray.

But tonight some color has returned. Our little one bustles hither and yon while Yongwon tells me that he asked a coworker for advice today, and the coworker advised him to update his résumé. "I didn't think that was an option," he confesses. "But after he said that, I felt like I could breathe again." I squeeze his hand. "Well, we told God we'd go wherever he leads. Where should I apply?"

We look at each other. The chapters of both our lives have always been divided by departures, and we are tired of moving. The chance to settle here in Colorado feels like an audacious request to make. But what do we have to lose? The God who guides us is free to say no.

We bow our heads. We ask to stay.

◇ ◇ ◇

I check the cardboard box in vain. *Ah, salt.* I've forgotten to bring salt for Yongwon's birthday dinner—our first meal in the first house we've ever owned, a little two-story structure in Colorado Springs. We won't move in until next month, so all my supplies are back at our rented house. From the kitchen sink I can see the front door, a few paces away; it's clear I didn't drop anything on the way in. I pause for a second to grin at the sight of little socked feet disappearing around the corner. The floor plan is ideal for keeping track of two children; no matter where they are, I'll be able to hear them from this spot.

The house itself is only twenty minutes from Yongwon's workplace, where he started his current job not long after our groundbreaking prayer three years ago. Settling here will be a new adventure, and I've been getting acquainted with all its features.

Meanwhile, the guests are about to arrive. The water for the spaghetti has come to a rolling boil and the orange almond salad is waiting to be tossed; basil and black pepper will have to provide enough seasoning for the tomato sauce on their own. Yongwon unfolds two Korean tables in the bare living room while the girls clamber up and down the stairs.

The doorbell rings. A cloud of merry voices wishes Yongwon a happy birthday before I can turn around from the stove. The two families we've invited tour the rooms and enter the kitchen, lured in by the savory smell of homemade meatballs. One friend dashes out to her car and returns with two disposable utensil kits, and, laughing, we sprinkle iodized salt from two tiny packets into the sauce before we scoop the meal onto paper plates.

"Don't worry about dropping food or leaving stains! The kids can eat anywhere they'd like." Yongwon and I have decided to replace the carpet here, which boasts marks of its faithful service to the former owners' two dogs and cat. The children might as well enjoy the freedom in the meantime. Watching them roam happily through the living room, one of the fathers grins and reclines back on his elbows.

The day the new carpet is installed, I slip over to the house after the girls' bedtime and vacuum each room, almost tiptoeing on the strange feel of unmatted plush tufts. When I finish, I sit down in the stairwell with my hand over my mouth. My parents have asked to pay for the carpet as a housewarming gift; I don't know how to thank them for this luxury.

Fresh color follows. The girls choose a light pink shade for their room, and Yongwon and I opt for a dusky blue to accent ours. During my growing-up years, my mother sewed curtains, hung frames, and chose furniture for the various apartments and houses where we lived, but she never painted the walls. This step feels momentous to me. It feels long-lasting.

Even with the pleasure of these improvements, however, I am surprised to discover how hesitant I am to let myself love this place. I tell myself I want to hold it loosely, knowing that the Lord I follow had "nowhere to lay his head" (Matt. 8:20; Luke 9:58). But if I'm honest, my stance is also a defense; a loose grasp will make things easier if a catastrophe strikes or we have to move on someday. I don't know if I am ready yet to regard it as more than a temporary holding, an event site in which to host others.

The week we move in, we dedicate the house to Christ through prayer. We pore over printouts of the floor plan and imagine how each room might welcome someone in the future: comforting meals in the kitchen, safe corners for people in need of a good cry or encouragement, perhaps a library someday in the loft. I want to be aware that this dwelling isn't wholly my own.

But as we unpack books and plates and toys, Corrie ten Boom enters my thoughts. A survivor of Ravensbruck concentration camp, Corrie traveled around the world for three decades speaking about Christ and giving her account of God's faithfulness to her family during World War II. Years into her ministry, a hostess in Colorado ushered her to a room with a stunning view of the mountains and told her that it would henceforth be set aside for her—a vibrant space to which Corrie could retreat and rest whenever she needed it. Corrie almost wept, floored by the gift of a room to call her own.[4] I ponder her reaction; even this stalwart woman was grateful for a physical, geographical anchor.

Jesus said, "In my Father's house are many rooms. If it were not so, would I have told you that I go to prepare a place for you?" (John 14:2). He did not choose to become the itinerant Son of Man because the concept of a home was inherently selfish or evil; rather, he left his place beside the Father in order to bring others into a Home that no person, disaster, or war would be able to take away. What might happen if I were to regard my temporary home as a place of belonging representative of his—a site worthy of attention, affection, and creativity?

I mull over this further as I come across authors who regard the arrangement and keeping of their own homes as modes of calling.[5] On paper I sketch out tentative traditions for our family of four and try out a dozen configurations of the photo frames we've collected through the years. Perhaps, after all, these have the potential to be more than mere activities and decorations. Perhaps they can be a scaffold on which little souls and aging ones can hang a secure sense of familial love, a gallery of the Father's faithfulness to look back on when their strength flags—within these rooms, upon this square of ground.

Late one night, Anthony Esolen sums up the tentative connection my mind is starting to make: "We have no abiding place

---

4. Corrie ten Boom, with Jamie Buckingham, *Tramp for the Lord* (Grand Rapids: Revell, 1974), 250–51.

5. The writings of Sally Clarkson, Sarah Clarkson, Edith Schaeffer, and Lanier Ivester have been especially inspiring and thought-provoking for me in this area.

on earth. But that does not mean that we are to love no place at all."[6]

◇ ◇ ◇

In the second summer we furrow lines in a small patch and sprinkle seeds: carrot, onion, basil, salvia, cosmos, snapdragon, pumpkin. Enthralled by the daily growth and bloom of their stretching green limbs during my afternoon rounds, I habitually forget to start dinner. Over time we will come to understand our plant hardiness zone and tailor our plans to the particular quirks of this plot; I have faith that we'll figure out how to lure the flea beetles away from the alyssum and coax flowers from the feathery cosmos bushes that are currently reveling in their adolescence.

These dreams of flourishing call back ancient words. "Build houses and live in them; plant gardens and eat their produce," God told the exiles who were carried away from Jerusalem to Babylon (Jer. 29:5). Their residence away from the city of their longing was not to be spent in barren despair. They had not fallen outside his plan; in fact, they were squarely in it. He would be with them in exile, too, as they sought the welfare of the place where he had sent them.

Is this what it means to love a spot on this earth, I wonder? Does it mean contemplating its strengths and flaws, its wounds and needs, in tandem with the One who has sent us here? More and more, I'm realizing that we're not merely in a house; we are in a neighborhood, a city, a county. Choosing to love our locality will

---

6. Anthony Esolen, introduction to *Nostalgia: Going Home in a Homeless World* (Washington, DC: Regnery Gateway, 2018), 35.

mean no longer regarding it as detached outsiders; it will mean thinking in terms of long-term effects and plans and relationships.

I am beginning to see how time and stationary presence can ground a transplant's mind, and how the kingdom of God can be built through incremental steps. In the spring, the four of us pry pebbles and elm roots as thick as our arms out of the dirt. Our patience burgeons as we work toward a growing vision of healing and cultivation year by year: this summer's garden budget will provide starter compost to fill the raised beds; next summer's will furnish some bricks for two low terracing walls. Indoors, we hang prints of Winslow Homer's *The Dinner Horn*, Monet's 1878 *The Parc Monceau*, and Childe Hassam's *The Water Garden*. We slide new and secondhand books onto sage green built-in shelves Yongwon has made and dream of touching the wick of conversation to their contents as the girls grow. I walk through the rooms as the seasons change, understanding that in these small ways we are staking a claim here—not to the mere material features in our care, but to our part in reflecting the mending work and patient beauty of our Creator.

In fifteenth-century Korea, an intricate system of beacons relayed news to the king.[7] Using dark, mugwort-tinged smoke by day and fire by night, lookouts along the seacoast passed messages via inland stations to a central beacon mound in the capital city. Two beacon fires warned of enemies sighted on the sea, three of their approach, four of their breach of the border or engagement with warships, and five of their landing or engagement with land

---

7. A system of signal fires had begun about 250 years prior; the beacon law was codified in the fifteenth century. The network of more than six hundred beacons continued to be used for five hundred years, until 1895.

troops.[8] But this line of communication did not only function during national emergencies. If there were no incidents to report, one beacon was lit to signal that all was well.

The act of stewarding an earthly house in the service of Christ is, I now believe, that single steady beacon. In times of exigency—family illness, local disaster, widespread war, persecution—every resource his people have must of course be mobilized for extraordinary use; each station always stands ready for the King's command. But in between these times (and one could well argue, especially during them) our temporary homes are concrete ways to affirm that "all shall be well, and all shall be well, and all manner of thing shall be well"[9]—that life is worth living as fully as we can and that we are not forsaken. When we tend our spaces with work and worship, however small or transitory those spaces may be, we join a pattern of bright stations that signal the way Home.

In this house and garden, I am learning what helps me fuel such a regular flame: simple routines built around listening for the Helper (John 14:26), a steward's investment of creativity, and the kind of unhurried attentiveness to sight and sound and texture that gives rise to thanks. Our rooms contain finished projects, tools, and objects that some may regard as "merely things," yes, but many of them are souvenirs of singular graces, from the rocking chair where I have held children through their feverish nights to the security camera box on the porch that sheltered a tiny house finch for an entire winter. Through these physical elements and

---

8. "The Ministry of War advises on the revised regulation for lighting the beacon fire," *The Veritable Records of King Sejong,* Year 1 (1419), Month 5, Day 26, Entry 9, accessed March 2, 2023, http://esillok.history.go.kr/record /recordView.do.

9. Julian of Norwich, *Revelations of Divine Love,* n.d.

the memories of mercy they bear, I am joined to the webbing of this particular place. Here I remember; here, I abide.

Love opens itself to the potential hurt of loss, gives itself to the task of holding out light. In the few years of tending this dwelling, I have given up the packable simplicity of an unmoored life.

◇ ◇ ◇

From the window seat in our little library, I can see over the rooftops of close-set houses. Today their gables point upward against a rare silver mizzle as my mind travels north on the road, surveying antelope herds on wide swaths of land that are being swallowed up daily by the maw of housing developments.

Fleet on the wings of my imagination, I enter the forest of ponderosa pines. A log cabin community center hails me like an old-time porch sitter, calling back fond memories of a Narnian Christmas party that the Anselm Society hosted there a few winters back. If I ever grow embittered and forgetful in old age, I hope to peek in its windows on a dreary night and espy the table laden with mince pies and cheeses and festal fare again, and beam at the hospitality of artists inviting their audience into snowy realms of story, song, and art. What an evening it was!

A few more miles beyond this landmark will bring me to the church where we attend Good Friday service every spring, since our own five-year-old church hosts no gathering on that day. But at the intersection I turn east instead, slowing to pass the ranch where we sometimes pick up pork shoulders and ground beef. Further east is the farm whose CSA shares gave us something to do during the quietest days of the pandemic in 2020: with no pressing engagements after we picked up our vegetables on Friday afternoons, we drove down random dirt roads and dipped into the hidden hollows of the countryside. Now we purchase our vegetable seedlings there.

Sweeping south, I pause where a grand old cottonwood used to stand by the side of the street until it was bulldozed. The landscape still seems strange without it. But I know the solace of a tree nursery a few miles away where baby crab apples, honey locusts, and fruit trees of all kinds stand straight in rows of promise year-round. We buy our Christmas tree from this nursery every November, and we've walked up and down the dusty aisles on different years, selecting a baby ginkgo and an elegant Sienna Glen maple to replace dying arboreal friends.

Then—only a stone's throw from the nursery is the hospital on the hill. Yongwon's father died in one of its rooms on a September morning, surrounded by peace and by family members. Here my thoughts always slow and still themselves, whether I am at this perch in the library or driving past the building on an errand. It is my personal *memento mori*: both a sobering reminder and a calming comfort to know that if we stay in this place, my own last breath will likely be taken somewhere amid these familiar spots. The part of me that is used to moving sounds a note of warning now and then: if we stay, we are bound to bid farewell to more friends, bound to witness the passing of more geographical features and events that perhaps no one else will remember. We will have to bear witness to the ravages of time.

But, ah, I see something further from my vantage point as well. I see the groundswell, the hidden ripples of a work running counter to the deterioration of a broken earth. Out on the farm, the owners envision not only a place to grow "beyond organic" heirloom produce; they are determined to restore the land. In their eyes it is not enough to leave the soil as it was; they want to nurture it to be richer than they found it—including the air and water that surround it. The ranch also takes a regenerative approach to its work. Resting on Audubon-certified land, it provides a safe habitat for grassland birds while raising cattle and pigs that, in turn, graze in ways that reduce the spread of invasive plants. Meanwhile, Christ followers I know are at work bridging the rift between the church and artists, praying for neighborhoods one street at a time, and finding ways to make sure schoolteachers and home educators feel supported.

Watching these people put their glad strength into the labor of mending brings me back to my own home and family with a tilted head and a renewed zest for dreams. Where should we put the ginkgo sapling where it will last long beyond our days? In what ways can we help to ease the suffering of other human beings? How can we encourage this painter or that poet? How can we acknowledge the ill and pass on the good of our family heritage? Where, today, can we take up an opportunity to love another with the quality of that abundant Love that has met us again and again? Maybe we can be a small sanctuary for a time. Maybe we can, as Wendell Berry says in a different story, "[help] a little the healing of the hurt world."[10]

The work of the kingdom is a long work, incremental growth from a tiny seed. It takes time and labor for yeast to work itself through dough, and our breadth of days hardly seems long enough

---

10. Wendell Berry, "The Art of Loading Brush," *The Threepenny Review* (Fall 2017), https://www.threepennyreview.com/samples/berry_f17.html.

to notice a change. Yes, this material world will undergo a fiery final phase. But by the mystery of a Homeward plan, the acts that are being sprinkled now, the practices being sown now, will bear fruit in the renewal of creation. Sons and daughters robust in creativity, delight, fortitude, endurance, imagination, and generosity will extend the kingdom of God over the whole of the new earth.

The good labor of working small visions into actuality has, to date, changed me so deeply that sometimes I wonder if my Lord was the One who planted the seed of that "prayer to stay" in our hearts in the first place. Perhaps we were not asking for permission to remain so much as we were asking him to put us to worthwhile work. Perhaps, when one brings a heart unbridled by expectation to him, the working out of his will is bound to feel like that: both permission and commission, an act of obedience and a gift of grace.

After twelve years, our homemaking and community-supporting efforts are still only a beginning. But it is a beginning that helps me grasp what the eternal God is bringing forth in a people who will shed their mortality as a sprouting seed sheds its husk.

From the kitchen on a Saturday afternoon, I look out at the hail cloth billowing like a sail under the shadows of our neighbors' elm tree, a sight as mesmerizing as sun pennies on the sea. The places under our care can be knit together through memory and meaning, invisible webs of a patient love interplaying and weaving and showing up clear in the right light. There is a richness that overlays itself a hundredfold, going down and out and sideways, as we learn to interlock with the netting of others' deeds and lives. For every act of cultivation and every thread of love spun in his name will outlive the brokenness. They herald something beyond what is possible now. This is our place to learn to mend, to restore what we can upon a finite earth, to live toward its remade form. I take in a breath. The place where we are now is our witness of what has been and our reminder, as Jayber says, of the future.

Of the world that is to come, and the World that is to come.

10

Through Pain

It starts with a stomachache. I am in the bathroom longer than I plan to be, and when I come back to the baby in her bassinet and her big sister among her books and puzzles, I wonder the usual: perhaps I ate something odd, or I picked up a stomach bug from the January buffet of viruses in town.

Only a brief pain, here and gone; against the backdrop of the past four months, it does not register as a major event. Last autumn I gave birth and soon afterward took our jaundiced newborn into the hospital for three days of treatment, which we expected. Two days after we came home, I spiked a fever and was admitted to a different hospital for an emergency appendectomy, which we did not expect. These days I am simply content to be home and doubly thankful for the absence of postpartum depression this time around.

Within thirty-six hours, however, the stomachache returns. After a third round later in the week and a fourth, it gains definition. It comes without warning at any time of day, starting from a low clenching in my abdomen and ramping up to pain of a severity that sends the other parts of my body into overdrive— cramping muscles, racing heartbeat, loss of temperature control, roiling digestion, and more. It lasts for almost exactly five hours each time. I can count on having a reprieve for at least twenty-four hours, but after that mark, I am a walking target for this unknown condition. Yongwon comes home from work one day to find me sitting on the kitchen floor, thumping my head backward onto a cabinet door in a steady beat to distract myself from the pain.

We adapt to this new development like people responding to phases of wildfire evacuation. The time I spend on the carpet, rolling toys to the baby and reading eagerly presented storybooks aloud to our little girl, is the first regular routine abandoned. Chores and plans laid with friends in better times are postponed again and again, piling up on the edges of the calendar like trinkets shunted aside in order to pack essentials. The change that hurts most is the one I notice well after it goes into effect: the hopeful requests for storybooks slow, and eventually stop altogether. On the day I cannot carry the baby ten steps across the room, the first day of many that I have to call Yongwon home from work, I know we have entered the next stage.

I report my symptoms to the doctor, listing every symptom I can think of that might be relevant. Times. Patterns. Body quadrants. A newfound deftness in description, ever elusive at the writing desk, settles on me like a curse. Organs that have operated for decades in my body without acclaim suddenly come under the scrutiny of a mind scrabbling for answers.

Lab orders and procedures take me on a circuitous tour of waiting rooms and their aquariums. Specialists check for an ulcer and for kidney stones. I schedule an endoscopy, pick up omeprazole, try supplements. In a fluorescent room wrapped like a vault behind layers of hallways and medical history questionnaires, I drink a box of chalky sweet liquid and watch as it filters through my gallbladder on a dark screen. A phlebotomist rolls up my sleeve to draw six tubes and inadvertently gasps; I glance down. The crook of my right arm has taken on the appearance of Orion's Belt: one unblinking red speck for each vein. Across town, a nurse practitioner hits my back with the side of her fist like a structural engineer testing the integrity of a wall. "Good," she pronounces. "You'd have yelled if it was your kidneys."

The pain in question never accompanies me into these places. Test after test comes back bafflingly clear, and I begin to look cheerful in an attempt to appear sane. An internal medicine doctor puts forward a hernia as his guess and creaks forward in his chair to add a parting word of advice: "*You* get to control your body. You get to tell it what to do, not the other way around." His tone is not unkind. I nod, lifting the corners of my mouth, and thank him for his time.

But during a dinnertime appointment, I walk through a deserted hallway into another exam room, and for a moment my expression breaks. The nurse pauses. She looks into my face, and for three seconds the world stops spinning askew as she reaches out to put a hand on my sleeve. "They'll figure out what it is," she says quietly. "It will be okay."

For those three seconds, and every time I think of her afterward, it almost doesn't matter if she is right; her gesture gives my waning hope a place to lean, to catch its breath.

I am deeply grateful for a primary care doctor who listens. I'm grateful for the medical knowledge and equipment that make it possible to rule out so many known conditions. All of the results should be reassuring for this closet hypochondriac, and they are—except that I go home to a specter it seems only I can sense.

Every pending test is a slow bloom of hope, however frail, until it blights. At home the pain ambushes me at unpredictable intervals, and in its wake creeps the silent suggestion that I may never again be healthy enough for the old rhythms. My dreams condense to a simple aspiration: I want only to be present as a wife and friend today, to be able to move about as a mother for the next twelve hours until the little ones can gently and lovingly be put to bed.

When I am alone, I wait in silence before my Creator, the One—right now, the only One—who knows the precise inner workings and frayed connections within this body. I know it is not the silence of absence. Somehow I know I am carried on the sustenance of life-giving words, unnoticed provisions, and three-second kindnesses. For we have many good days too: Yongwon gives me a haircut for the first time, and we grin over the outcome; on Valentine's Day, I slip a dress of red rosettes over my firstborn's delighted head and send her out to lunch with Daddy. But in between I brace for the uncertainty, the weakness, the vigilance that severs me from the active land of the living.

One night I wake at 2:00 a.m. to the gallop of a cardiac stampede in my ears. My muscles contract with relentless force, hijacked by a command my brain cannot intercept, until my shoulder and hip bones feel like they are caving in toward my crumpling core. I have been waiting for a doctor to tell me how much worse things might get, but no second opinion is needed for the dead certainty that comes to me now. Something is going to buckle permanently under this kind of pressure, and soon.

◊ ◊ ◊

The aroma of breakfast sausage frying coaxes me awake. By the time I slip into a chair at the kitchen table, Yongwon has finished cooking the last omelet, which he slides onto my plate with a flourish. I laugh. Breakfast beams up at me: Italian sausage eyes, a slivered bell pepper nose, an exceedingly wide yellow smile stuffed with vegetables. Between bites of omelet and sips of strong black tea, I listen to our three-year-old's Saturday plans for her stuffed baby zebra and Yongwon's work news from the week.

How hungry I am for time. After two months of asking to be excused from the table and from relationships and from life, every hour is a windfall put toward making up lost laughter and missed meals. A pang choked my throat last night when I looked at the baby monitor and saw that our newborn now fills up half of her crib—when did this happen? The last time I looked, she was a tiny bundle lost in its expanse. An undercurrent of prayer hums through my mind like an urgent and wary liturgy: *Let it be a good morning—a good afternoon—a good evening. Please.*

But by midmorning, it is clear this will not be a day of recompense. Yongwon glances at the pallor of my face and brushes his hand over the damp chill setting in upon its edges. He takes the baby from my arms. "You should go upstairs and lie down."

I walk upstairs, defeated. I know it will be better to emerge, spent, in the afternoon than to lie on the couch snagging the activity of an otherwise happy household. I curl myself around my open laptop and a stack of books on the bed and wait for the crescendo.

Online, a friend has shared a video of a song; I click on it listlessly.

"When the Saints," by Sara Groves, starts with a roll and a spirited drumbeat—a call to attention as the vocalized murmur of a background chorus rises in harmony. I catch none of these details the first time it plays. I don't think I have it in me to respond to the rousing pace, but the lyrics begin to scroll up from the bottom of the screen. Two phrases glint: "heavy burden," "more than I can handle." Sara's voice is neither smooth nor glib here, and soon I am listening.

A chord catches me off guard. The next lines continue: "And when I'm weary and overwrought / With so many battles left unfought / I think of Paul and Silas in the prison yard . . ."[1] These words redirect my thoughts. I think I recognize most of the saints in the stanzas that follow, and for an instant my concentration lingers, one at a time, on Harriet Tubman, Elisabeth Elliot, and Mother Teresa.

When the song ends, I play it again. And right as the pain in my middle squeezes and holds, my perspective shifts.

Up to this point, I have been viewing myself as a figure on an island of pain, irrelevant to those who cannot share it; a dot floating anchorless in significance and time. All the guessing, hoping,

---

1. Sara Groves, "When the Saints," © 2008 Sara Groves Music. This material has been copied with the copyright holders' permission. Further reproduction, distribution, or transmission is prohibited, except as otherwise permitted by law.

and waiting for a resolution has taken place within the confines of my life—so much activity within, so little connection to anything without. But as I consider the saints, my mental range of sight widens to see above and outside that dot, so that my life is no longer an isolated incident but one in a long thread of small but radiant existences stretching backward and forward through history.

This is the line and lineage of believers, I know. This great cloud of witnesses to which more are being added daily, all moving Homeward—none of them are strangers to pain or loss or suffering. Keller points out the undeniable trait woven into the heredity of the Christian faith:

> We want the storyline of our lives to go from strength to strength, from success to success, and end happily ever after. But throughout the Bible we see something completely different—a persistent narrative pattern of life through death or of triumph through weakness that reveals how God works in history and in our lives.[2]

These saints, these believers, walk in the knowledge that the most enduring kind of joy is often bought with weakness—that weakness itself can be a catalyst that moves imperishable gain from the seen to the unseen realm.

There on the bed, I think of these children and women and men streaming into the kingdom so intently that it seems as if I could reach out and touch them as they pass, and the reality of what the Bible says becomes almost palpable. Its statements are

---

2. Timothy Keller, *Hope in Times of Fear: The Resurrection and the Meaning of Easter* (New York: Viking, 2021), 66.

nothing to be trifled with: the first will be last and the last will be first (Matt. 19:30; Mark 10:31; Luke 13:30). Those whom we would deem most deserving of our pity now are those who will receive the greater measure of honor when the kingdom of God comes in fullness. God "does not forget the cry of the afflicted" (Ps. 9:12); he is the unfailing champion of the fatherless, the widow, the sojourner (Ps. 68:5; Ps. 146:9; Deut. 10:17–18), the bankrupt in spirit (Matt. 5:3). If the upside-down honor of the kingdom proves true, the people I know who are suffering greatly will be miles upon miles ahead of me if the saints ever do "go marching" in a single procession. Their stories, in many ways, have spelled out to me the compassion and mercy and faithfulness of God in situations where I did not think his presence could be evident. They will be among the company who declare that the love they have received from him is worthy of their all.

This view sets my own pain in context amid decades, centuries, eons. I do not have control over the world events I will live through or the gauntlets I will have to run, but like these Christ followers scattered throughout the ages, I have this day's chance to be faithful. To trust God "where [I] cannot trace him."[3] The chorus of the song loops around again: "And when the Saints go marching in / I want to be one of them."[4] *Yes.* Something in me

3. Charles Spurgeon, "A Happy Christian," The Spurgeon Center for Biblical Preaching at Midwestern Seminary, 1867, accessed March 3, 2023, https://www.spurgeon.org/resource-library/sermons/a-happy-christian.

4. Sara Groves, "When the Saints," © 2008 Sara Groves Music. This material has been copied with the copyright holders' permission. Further reproduction, distribution, or transmission is prohibited, except as otherwise permitted by law.

flutters beyond the grip of pain and opens its wings to the air current of Home again. *I want to be one of them.*

In Marilynne Robinson's *Gilead,* John Ames writes: "In eternity this world will be Troy, I believe, and all that has passed here will be the epic of the universe, the ballad they sing in the streets. Because I don't imagine any reality putting this one in the shade entirely, and I think piety forbids me to try."[5] My opportunity in this world is, in the end, a brief one. The days of mortals are but "a few handbreadths" (Ps. 39:5), but what we do here will matter for eternity. Our triumphs. Our hidden and sacrificial acts of love, kept as secret as the deeds of one hand concealed from the other. Our endurance in trial, of which Paul said, "This light momentary affliction is preparing for us an eternal weight of glory beyond all comparison" (2 Cor. 4:17). This is the prelude, and within it ring the themes of the full-blown beauty of the restoration.

For one startling moment, in which I see perhaps more clearly than I ever have, it seems like so little to trade for so much.

As the song continues to play, my thoughts turn toward a certain paralyzed man who was brought to Jesus by his friends. Looking up the parallel passages in the Gospels, I read in three of them that Jesus sees the faith of the friends and says to the man, "Your sins are forgiven" (Matt. 9:2; Mark 2:5; Luke 5:20). Mark and Luke note that the friends have dismantled the roof in order to reach Jesus.

I can understand their determination. What a relief it would be to haul my own tired form down into a village to see the Son of God in the flesh. Lacking the boldness to tunnel my way to him, however, I would probably haunt the dusty road and wait until I

---

5. Marilynne Robinson, *Gilead* (New York: Picador, 2006), 57.

could surreptitiously sweep my fingertips across the fringe of his garment—but I shake my head and return to the page. Men have made a hole in the ceiling for their friend. *It could not be clearer* that the paralytic has been brought to Jesus for physical healing.

They present him to the miraculous healer. In the next breath he could say, "Rise and walk," with the authority to which every skeletal muscle cell and sea tempest in creation is subject, but he looks at this man and his determined fellowship first.

And then, in a sequence that strikes me to the heart, Christ does respond to the paralyzed man's greatest need.

"Take heart, my son; your sins are forgiven" (Matt. 9:2).

This, of all the things he could speak into being. But now I see.

Jesus tends to this man in such a way that the man will never need to be crippled by doubt over whether his goodness will suffice when his dust finally settles to the dust of the earth.[6] He sets him free from the regrets of his past, the failings of his future, and all the arresting fears of the present. Whether the man's feet lie limp or support his steps in the world, he is invited to dance without condemnation in the next—the life that shall make this one look

---

6. I chose the word *tends* here as a simple description of Christ's action, but Tish Harrison Warren gives deeper insight into the word within the context of (Anglican) Compline prayer: "Tending implies serving another, shepherding them, providing for their needs. It requires care, attention, and compassion. . . . [T]ending certainly may involve healing. But we are asking for more here than for God to simply show up like a physician and make the sick well. This [Compline] prayer has the audacity to ask that the God of the universe would stoop not only to heal us but to care for us, to nurse us in our most unimpressive states. We need God to bring wholeness to our souls, even through the brokenness of our bodies" (Tish Harrison Warren, *Prayer in the Night* [Downers Grove, IL: InterVarsity Press, 2021], 100).

like a "puff of air" and "shadows in a campfire" (Ps. 144:4 MSG). The Lord of life loves him, and he does not heal him physically, at least not in this initial moment, not until the scribes grumble. First he heals him in the way he needs it most.

With this thought, a sudden, almost unbearable joy crashes down on me like a deluge—undiluted, untainted, unthreatened. The weight of the coming glory outstrips the afflictions of the present, welling up and flooding over, and I weep brokenly as the crushing burden of uncertainty washes away.

Once, in reference to postpartum depression, I scribbled: "Even when you hit rock bottom, he is there." The statement has bothered me through the years. Certainly it is true, but the experience I spoke from then was like standing in a dark enclosure and blinking as the light was turned on. My confidence came from finding myself suddenly in a bright space and construing that someone must have been there with me all along.

But on this Saturday, I lie in a dark room and know without reaching out that someone is here: One who will not let me go, whose sovereignty is absolute and whose love never fails. The light does not need to be turned on, and incredibly, I do not require a promise that it will be. I am loved by and held in the gaze of my God, sealed by his Spirit for the day of redemption (Eph. 4:30), and though I cannot see a way forward, I lack nothing.

The pain is ebbing. I glance up at the laptop screen, propped sideways near my head. I've typed out halting, ungraceful fragments with my right arm pinned under me, trying to spell out the truth I perceive, as I perceive it, in this unclouded minute. To remember.

I am . . . tasting the richness of being wrenched from my daily everything. Looking out on a (possible) life of having episodes like this and not feeling bleak.

He has reminded me again that my life is not a single reel of fighting to get better, and perhaps getting there, or perhaps not. It is part of a long view, a history of saints whom I hope to join as they come marching into eternity declaring the all-sufficiency of God.

Today I know this for sure, in the core of my soul, more solidly than I have ever known it all my life.

I cannot be taken out of the love of God.

He is sufficient for my every area of life, more than sufficient, and I am rich in Christ, in whom I find my every need met, my Very Present Help available at all times. And I who cannot escape this pain, for now at least, find it not my fetter but my lifeline today that frees me from believing that this life is about being well and performing well.

He is trustworthy, Love in its purest form, my all-sufficient grace at all times.

At all times.

◇ ◇ ◇

The episodes continue to come and go, and then unexpect-edly disappear for a week. I meet a friend for brunch and order a slice of quiche. Three hours after returning home I am shivering under a blanket. *Could it be eggs?*

I meet with an allergist for a full-scale test. The egg sample comes out negative, and the allergist herself is dubious because of the varying length of time that passes between digestion and reac-tion. Still, she remarks, "If it's true, that would be fascinating. I'd want to write a paper about you." If it's true, then the intolerance would have begun right after my second labor and delivery.

The strongest evidence comes by trial: after I eliminate eggs, the episodes cease. I figure out more over time: miniscule amounts are permissible, especially if baked; larger amounts are not. The memory of the pain is still vivid enough, and reinforced by the occasional mistake, that I lack motivation to explore it further.

Since that tentative resolution, new diagnoses unrelated to the egg intolerance have arrived. I have "won" so many EKGs that I've thought about asking for a punch rewards card: qualify for four tests, get the fifth one free. During my yearly cardiology checkup, I often grin at the banter outside my exam room door; I never knew there were so many quick-witted seventy-year-olds in my town. Monitoring my insulin resistance, I learn how to draw blood from my fingertips so that it doesn't hurt; I track dates for my endocrine disorder and dysautonomia in hopes that I might know when to expect chills and impaired hearing and heart rate spikes. In the meantime, I talk with friends who are on oxygen, friends with stage-four cancer, and friends with babies in intensive care. They remind me repeatedly that it is wise not to discount the pain in one life by comparing it to another's.

"Everyone's got something," as my parents and doctor say. I don't believe the fractured mystery of my physical form is exceptional. But sometimes, for an honest minute, I stare at the wall or at a spot beyond the bathroom mirror, weary. On long nights I whisper prayers horizontally and get up to sift pain from anxiety, to sweat symptoms out, or to see what I can use from the mental toolbox that a counselor once helped me pack. I try to remember it is absolutely a right thing, a good thing, to persist in asking for all kinds of healing, for I have a body in addition to a soul.

These new health conditions and the distance of years sometimes make that long-ago pain seem very small. In the end, it took up only two months of my life. And what is two months? Today I read the words I wrote while crumpled that Saturday and quail to share them because they sound almost too idealistic and naïve— and yet I find I cannot erase them. I remember I had nothing to prove when I wrote them, as well as nothing to offer, and I was filled.

The blind man in John 9 stated what he knew to be true: "One thing I do know, that though I was blind, now I see" (v. 25). Like the plain evidence of his sight, the concentrated joy I tasted is a simple fact I can't explain and can only affirm. I have carried the memory of it within me through the subsequent years as proof that my Lord's signposts of joy also exist in valleys of suffering, where they gleam like streetlamps in the night. Even there, he walks beside us, behind us, and before us, leading the way.

And I hold up this instance of joy-amid-pain as a torch sometimes, like fire borrowed from Home, like an ancient flame passed down from ages past, to answer the weariness that sometimes feels like it can destroy the marrow of my bones. I have both a body and a soul, make no mistake. But one of these will last beyond the other in its present form. One of them in particular is only a shadow of what it will be, and I want my soul to inform my body of the unbridled healing that is coming for it—the wholeness of the resurrection that will clothe it with indomitable joy.

Someday I expect to dash down the streets in the city of the saints without needing to pause for palpitations. I will see the Lamb of God, but not as one who shrinks back, and not from afar. And this bright signpost I have carried all these years—this aid that has enabled me to follow the outline of his figure in valleys past comprehending—I will lay it down at its Source finally, a candle to the sun.

11

As a Writer

A bag of provisions, a tattered pouch of seeds, five shooting stars made from the extract of an extinct flower: the boy takes only what is necessary into a dying land.

Though it is the end of summer, a chill wind blows from the east. The boy has no map, but he knows his destination will not be hard to find if he keeps walking toward the source of that wind. For many days and nights he travels, and the sky grows more ill-tempered and ashen the farther he goes.

More frightening than anything he sees is what he hears as he trudges onward. When the darkness thickens so that he can barely make out shapes around him and his eyes begin to invent shapes of their own, he hears voices trapped in that endless night. They are the voices of those who have lost their homes, refugees from thorn-carpeted regions scrabbling toward places where the sun still rises.

Shivering, he hears cries of pain that go unanswered because each traveler is isolated by private terrors. He hears the brittle breathing of people who pass each hour wondering what fresh calamity will visit them next. The air in every direction churns with the sound of suffering, and the boy grieves, grieves as he has not known he could.

Then he hears a child, keening in loneliness.

The boy halts. He knows this sound as if it comes from his own past: fractured, rootless, lost. He staggers toward the voice, reaching out with his arms, but the sobs seem to come from right and left at once. His lips are too stiff and cracked to form words; each breath blizzards out and sprinkles to the ground in crystal grains. For a minute he stands still in the dark.

Or does he?

I furrow my brow and blink long, trying to trace the boy's movements through a mental muddle. Yesterday I took my first draft of this story to the monthly meeting of the Anselm Arts Guild. My reading of it at the end of the night showed it for what it was: a patchwork of pieces without an immediately coherent design. I know I have some resewing and serging to do before I present it to a larger group at a public event tonight.

Sharing a rough draft with peers was a new experience for me. I watched them try to follow the story, their facial expressions offering excellent feedback in themselves. I wasn't sure what I wanted to hear at the end, but their tentative suggestions have had a few hours to sink in, and the echoes of their comments are shaping the story now, in a process I'm learning to embrace.

When I was small, I made up stories and—especially when I could find a participant willing to undergo all their peril and drama—I acted them out. Books of all kinds stretched my sense of compassion and empathy throughout childhood and made my imagination "capacious," as Kate DiCamillo would say.[1] At home, words and the many tapestries they formed were encouraged; somehow my mother made generous room in the budget for Scholastic book orders, and my little brother usually accepted my recommendations. "You'll like this one," I would assure him, passing him a volume by E. B. White or Gertrude Warner. "You can toss it across the room if you don't like it by the third chapter, but I'm pretty sure you'll want to keep reading." Later I'd peek around the corner to find him absorbed in its pages. My father, meanwhile, kept a pair of English-Korean and Korean-English dictionaries by his side. If he came across an unfamiliar word in a book or paper or movie, he would look it up within those onionskin pages and sometimes go the rest of the day repeating it so that he could get used to the proper pronunciation.

As I grew, I came to understand that one could not only tell a story but also persuade others through writing, whether through personal letters or college application answers or essays. In college I gravitated to literature classes, but the class that ultimately taught me the most about honing a clear and attractive argument wasn't in the English department; it was a Korean history course for which I had to write two-page papers. "That's all the space you get; don't waste a word," the professor warned us. When I got my first assignment back, I saw he had marked the sections where I had been redundant, and I respected him all the more for it. This kind of training continued into a graduate program in English

---

1. Kate DiCamillo, "Newbery Medal Acceptance Speech," Newbery Caldecott Banquet, American Library Association Annual Conference, June 28, 2014, https://www.ala.org/alsc/sites/ala.org.alsc/files/content/awardsgrants/bookmedia/newbery-14.pdf.

where I learned not so much how to write more eloquently as to *think* more clearly, which was the groundwork I needed for better writing.

In all that time, however, I remained wary about giving anything I wrote in draft form to someone else for comment. Even when I became a mother and began writing small sketches, most of them went into an unknown online journal. These snippets were certainly not academic in any sense; they simply existed to help me be more present in my own daily life. When the snippets expanded into stories and essays and submissions, I wrote them in what spare time I could squirrel away and did not presume them to be anything more than a hobby.

But in January of this year, I finally paused and asked my Lord what I ought to do. The question arose, thankfully, within a season of contentment; I held it freely, open to the possibility that he might direct me to other endeavors in this chapter of life. I asked if I should be using my time in a different way.

The answer, so far as I could discern it, surprised me. Like small waves nudging the tide up the shoreline, articles I encountered over the course of a month—principally through the website of The Rabbit Room—kept resounding upon the same theme. The theme was neither "you have a gift; take it up to bless the world," nor "write if you must, but indulge only after all other tasks and duties are complete"; instead, over and over I seemed to be reminded that I was a part of the body of Christ and that, as such, I had a call to live and breathe and *be*. The pieces I read introduced me to the notion that a vocation might not be an intimidating and lofty charge after all, but an allotment plot given to me to tend faithfully—a small square of a harvest field in which to grow and give out what I could.

Thus I seemed to have my answer, but part of it still lay blank. *All right,* I asked him again, *if I've heard you correctly, then—write what?*

One evening, upon looking up an oft-quoted passage from *Mere Christianity,* I read on and found words that struck me like a thunderclap. "I must keep alive in myself the desire for my true country, which I shall not find till after death," Lewis wrote, "I must never let it get snowed under or turned aside; I must make it the main object of life to press on to that other country and to help others to do the same."[2] These words plucked the note to which my life and heart had already been tuned, and the force of their resonance seemed to clear a path of glad direction before me. Here, what I had that passed for a skill set fused with the Homeward longing that was coming into clarity.

So I gave the writing over, surrendering it, and asked God to use it as he would. The result has since surprised me. Since that point of review, an unmistakable change has spread into the way I approach writing.

I have been learning to love the reader more, for one.[3] The practice of writing, it seems, is not exempt from the two greatest commandments.[4] The small choices I make with words—the flow

---

2. C. S. Lewis, *Mere Christianity* (New York: HarperSanFrancisco, 1952, rev. ed. 2001), 137.

3. This is one of the constant emphases of Jonathan Rogers's *The Habit* weekly newsletter and *The Habit* podcast—two invaluable resources that have helped to shape much of my growth as a writer. Accessed March 3, 2023, https://thehabit.co.

4. James E. Beitler III and Richard Hughes Gibson's *Charitable Writing* (Downers Grove, IL: IVP Academic, 2020), uses art, metaphor, historical

and tone, the balance between Anglo-Saxon and Latinate terms—
are a matter of hospitality, even when the result is not everyone's
cup of tea. At the desk, I've released "some of the things that char-
acterize my life now—the concern over what other people will
think, the self-protective cautiousness, the reserve that keeps me
from being fully engaged."[5] I cannot serve from a life that is safely
clasped shut. And every day a little piece of paper in a cubbyhole
reminds me to "go one step further" for the reader, to try to add
something worthwhile to the agelong discourse on a given topic
rather than writing simply to be heard.

I've also become more willing to edit and revise written pieces,
sometimes stripping them back completely to their basic frames
and starting again. Sometimes it takes a while to find the right
form for the work; sometimes the decision depends on what will
suit a particular audience best. Whatever shape it eventually takes,
the eyes of others help me examine the writing from more angles
than I could see on my own. In *The Company They Keep,* a book
about the Inklings and their interactive community, Diana Glyer
writes that "the power of editors to affect a text depends on how
fixed or fluid the writer considers the text to be."[6] As my perspective on writers in community changes, I'm learning to hold my
drafts loosely. Inviting the input of friends, contrary to what I
once thought in my vague discomfort, is not a call for them to

---

anecdotes, and practical suggestions to illustrate how writers can engage in
their work as part of their Christian discipleship. I've found it is well worth
revisiting at regular intervals.

5. Carolyn Arends, *Wrestling with Angels* (Eugene, OR: Harvest House,
2008), 190.

6. Diana Glyer, *The Company They Keep: C. S. Lewis and J. R. R. Tolkien
as Writers in Community* (Kent, OH: Kent State University Press, 2007), 102.

find all the faults in my words; it is a request to help me make those words as clear and well expressed as I can.

Most of all, I've been paying more attention to what praise and rejection can do to me. Intentionally keeping company with my husband and friends as they go about their own work keeps my perspective on stable ground. The longer I work in a culture in which writers, artists, and musicians are counseled to adopt this strategy or that one for successful public engagement, the more I realize that in all this striving I do not want to be disqualified from the real race I am running (1 Cor. 9:27).

To that end, small communities like the Anselm Guild and the Cultivating Project have provided a lifeline of camaraderie and prayer. Through them, I've met people whom I have come to trust—who know what I am trying to do not merely with this short fiction piece but all my work. I understand that we are invested in helping one another's work become more coherent and alive, and I've seen firsthand that works in progress come into fuller beauty under the shelter of such fellowship.

Everything, in short, is different. I type the concluding words of my short story, frame it fore and aft as a formal toast addressed "to the King's council," and add the line that Teressa suggested at the end of the guild meeting: "Thank you for the courtesy of your audience." It is only as I save and close the document that I realize the words are as much for my guild colleagues as they are for the imaginary people gathered within the tale.

◇ ◇ ◇

That evening, I read the story aloud to a full room.

My voice quavers until it settles into the momentum of the piece. When I reach the site where the boy stands unmoving in the black cold, we pause together, narrator and protagonist, garnering a breath for what will follow.

Without hesitation he reaches into his pack and sends up a shooting star. Then another, and another, and another, for the sake of that solitary soul in the wilderness. They blaze overhead, and in their brief arc of light, he can see no one around him, but he hears the weeping no more after that.

He walks on into the heart of the story with one priceless star left, and I keep one eye on my audience. I cannot see their expressions clearly, but I hope earnestly that I have given them space to enter into this country and walk with the boy, free from any impulse to diagram his journey in allegorical terms. I hope I have hosted them well.

I finish reading and escape off the low stage, letting the tension slough off my shoulders as I tiptoe back to my seat. The theme of the evening is, appropriately, "Storytelling." Stefani, another artist, closes the program by sharing custom-made seed packets and encouraging us to tend the stories inherent in our names. Glancing around the room, I think back upon Evangeline's ghostly folktale and Teressa's songs, drawn from her family life, and I watch faces glow in the reflection of these shared worlds.

Afterward, a few listeners ask me where they can find the story about the boy. When I tell them it is part of a larger story I have in mind, they look me square in the eye and say, "Good. *Please finish it.*"

The setting and the generous intensity of the audience work their magic. As I mull over the experience in the days that follow,

I realize that after all these years I am returning to the form that drew me to words in the first place. This is where my heart meets the work I want to offer with my hands: telling stories in order to help others move Homeward. I do not mean, of course, "telling stories" as falsehoods, but telling them as a means of seeing truth illuminated and scattered into life until every nook and cranny are filled with a lively gladness; I mean telling stories as a way of imparting an *atmosphere* that moves and fills the reader with a heightened sensibility akin to the effect of unforgettable music. Stories are the avenue through which I've been moved in my own life and spurred along in my faith. Their influence testifies to a property of art spelled out by Malcolm Guite: "Works of imagination are not . . . reducible to private or subjective worlds. The way a living artist imagines, or reimagines, the world—remythologizes the world—actually affects the way we perceive the world itself, often for the better."[7] Within me, a steady aspiration rises to tell nonfiction and fiction narratives that might help others "press on" to their true country.

But I am a different storyteller from the one I would have been, I know, had I not stopped to ask my Lord what he thought. The exchange of that question and answer have brought about at least three foundational gifts.

First, I am freed by the awareness that I am working alongside others in the kingdom. It is not my task to make an entire comprehensive argument for the gospel—with history, etymology,

---

7. Malcolm Guite and Judith Wolfe, "Creation and New Creation in J. R. R. Tolkien and C. S. Lewis" in *The Art of New Creation: Trajectories in Theology and the Art,* Jeremy Begbie, Daniel Train, and W. David O. Taylor, eds. (Downers Grove, IL: InterVarsity Press, 2022), 163.

exegesis, apologetics, political implications, pop culture connections, poetic expression—in my work. I *am* called to tell the truth,
in as whole a form as possible, as deeply as possible, but I will not
convey it in every possible mode, just as I would not use charcoal
and colored pencils and watercolor and acrylic paint together as a
visual artist. "Most of us are under pressure, external or internal,
to do everything, be good at everything, be accountable to everyone for everything!" laments Guite in *The Word in the Wilderness.*
"It is not so. In the divine economy each of us has a particular grace, gift and devotion."[8] I am the beneficiary of artists and
authors who have known this truth. Leif Enger's *Peace like a River,*
Marilynne Robinson's *Gilead,* Elizabeth Goudge's *Green Dolphin
Street,* and Susanna Clark's *Piranesi* are novels as different from
one another as cuisines across the world, but each one has taught
me something about beauty, fidelity, and home. Witnessing such
a range makes me glad to be in the company of other saints, and
it gives me vim to press onward in carrying out my own part in
the great relay.

Second, I'm heartened to know that our vocations will not
end with death. Tish Harrison Warren points out that work itself
will be redefined when the curse of the fallen earth is no more:

> In the eschatological reality we watch for, work
> itself will be made new. Isaiah 65 speaks of God
> creating a new heaven and new earth, where
> labor will no longer be marked by toil. It's not
> that we will no longer work. . . . Instead, God's

---

8. Malcolm Guite, *The Word in the Wilderness: A Poem a Day for Lent and
Easter* (Norwich: Canterbury Press, 2014), 79.

people "shall long enjoy the work of their hands"
(Isaiah 65:22). None of us will labor in vain.[9]

I can hardly envision work apart from toil and resistance, but it gives me a wave of sober delight to consider what it might be like to craft using willing materials as an amateur watercolor artist, a singer, a gardener, a cook. I'll have a long time to learn.

As a writer, I will not need to help others keep the hope of their true country foremost *there*. Sometimes I wonder if the stories we tell in the new creation will keep to the same narrative structures we use here and now. Surely many of them will, since the central history of our salvation and the gospel of Christ has set us a sure pattern, but I would venture to guess there are dimensions even to storytelling that we may yet encounter—new dimensions of meaning, themes, and phases that we do not have the ability to receive or evoke today. Yet even based on what I know, I look forward to someday telling stories to faces who have beheld the Love that courses through the center of this universe and who delight to see some aspect of him unfolded again before their eyes, like a lover discovering some hitherto unknown gift or hidden deed of the beloved. Who can say what he might do to bring such stories to ripeness then?

Third, and the greatest surprise thus far, the journey of creating something under the guidance of the Master Artist is turning out to be a journey of learning rhythms, matching paces, laughing ruefully at my bumbling missteps, and venturing outward for an occasional twirl. I've often heard artists quote Eric Liddell's

---

9. Tish Harrison Warren, *Prayer in the Night* (Downers Grove, IL: InterVarsity Press, 2021), 69.

declaration that he felt the pleasure of God while running; for me, the exhilaration comes from partnering with the Lord with pen in hand and receiving the kind of training wherein my sovereign Instructor clearly goes before me.

For nothing is wasted. I have flinched in empathy, encouraged, to read of authors who had to stop work to mow the lawn or to recover from postholiday gloom or to take a child to the doctor. But I've also begun to notice that my own interruptions and duties often shape the next sentence I need to write by adjusting my frame of mind; one day's derailments enrich the writing of the next day's portion. Somehow the work is carried along. The word *inspire* is descended from the Latin *inspirare*, meaning "blow into, breathe upon,"[10] and indeed, the movement from snippets to sketches to drafts feels as though it is sustained by breaths given moment by moment. Wiser minds than mine are better acquainted with this pattern that has taken me years to notice and additional years to settle into without fear.[11]

These days, at the outset of a project, I pray for sound lines of thought, and the words that will carry those thoughts. A little while later I pray for the willingness to produce rickety first drafts and the sheer perseverance to put up with the tedious sound of my written voice. I look up definitions to words I thought I knew and am abashed to find I've had them all wrong. As it comes together, I pray that the work will, trickling or fluttering, find its way to the right reader, and I remember what a privilege it is if this

---

10. *Online Etymology Dictionary*, s.v. "inspire," accessed September 9, 2022, https://www.etymonline.com/search?q=inspire.

11. Andrew Peterson's *Adorning the Dark* (Nashville: B&H, 2019) gives an honest, detailed account of his experience with doubt and courage as a songwriter and author.

should happen to be a single reader. Then I have amnesia about the entire process and come rusty to the drawing board again for the next assignment, wondering if the supply of mercy will run out this time.

But my Lord has answered these prayers so many times, and so thoroughly, that over the years I think I can see how his patient teaching is changing me. Every so often I can hear the rightness of a phrase in the way it lands on my ear. Sometimes an over-throttled sentence shouts at me to leave it unfinished, with blanks, so that I can return to it later; sometimes I put away a document entirely if a reorienting pause seems necessary. Insight comes in fits and starts. As a consequence, if a kind word later arrives from a reader in response to something I've finished, I remember clearly the bankruptcy of having to ask God for help at every stage, and I know for certain that the credit does not lie wholly with me.

The open page, blank or crowded, is where I am learning to wait for him. Vocations can shift; he is still free to redirect me, or to lead me in this one differently. But meanwhile I am discovering what it is to sing the song he has put in my mouth (Ps. 40:3), as David says; this is how I am telling stories Homeward.

◇ ◇ ◇

So I show up to a small writing desk by an icy window late on a November evening. In the winter the wall radiates a chill that will seep into my right arm—a chill I will not notice until my fingers stiffen over the keyboard—so I begin by scooting to the left edge of the work surface. I swaddle my hands around a mug of tea and resume my stance as a furtive follower.

I trail this boy and his family through winding mountain passes, into the realm of a story that keeps expanding beyond my capacity. I try to learn their names and track what they have undertaken, despite the gravelly frustrations and obscuring boulders that come along.

For what else can I do? My time is limited, as it is for all humans. But I hear the keening around me, and I know something of a love that brings the light of a future hope and a present calling. Like the boy at its center, I do not know who will see this tale, or if it will be of use to anyone at all. But for the sake of the One who attends me—I send up my flare in the dark.

12

While Fighting the Good Fight

How wise is it to think aloud in front of someone you've just met?

I am sitting at a patio table across from a classmate on our college campus. Our conversation hasn't stopped since we sat down to our lunch; she is warm and gregarious and seems like the kind of person who might make an excellent friend. After establishing that we share similar tastes in books, she has volleyed up a whimsical icebreaker of a question: "Which character do you identify with most from *The Lord of the Rings*?"

In response, I am hesitating.

The name I want to give isn't the name I probably should give. Yet who cares? Courtesy tells me I should simply pick one and let our discussion move on. But her question has cracked a door in my thoughts ajar, and I sense there is something beyond it that matters deeply to me, something that has challenged my continual striving and left me with an impression sweeter and nobler than I can name.

But how much of this should I say to my lunch companion? This is hardly small talk; it's the kind of conversation you subject close friends to, in small and humane amounts. For a sober few seconds, I deliberate. I decide to risk following my train of thought in front of this person who may very well finish her chicken sandwich in a hurry and remember a forgotten appointment.

"I'd like to say Arwen, but I think I ought to say Éowyn," I say finally, strongly tempted to plant my face in my empty food container. Miraculously, she leans in. I push on the door, tiptoe into Middle-earth, and begin a yearslong journey of unwrapping the implications of my claim.

◇ ◇ ◇

J. R. R. Tolkien's *The Lord of the Rings* is a tender spot for me, marking a paradigm shift in my understanding of the world that came at seventeen. Written in the years spanning 1937 to 1949,[1] the book is the most well-known of Tolkien's works and one that I initially read with hesitation. After following hobbits on an exhaustive trek through much of *The Fellowship of the Ring, The Two Towers* lay stubbornly untouched on my desk for six months; I lost the motivation to keep reading when I realized that Tolkien was not going to cut back and forth between his two main groups of travelers. But something in the tale kept drawing me back, a

---

1. "Tolkien began *The Lord of the Rings* in December of 1937, and he completed the typescript in 1949" (Diana Glyer, *Bandersnatch: C. S. Lewis, J. R. R. Tolkien, and the Creative Collaboration of the Inklings* [Kent, OH: Black Squirrel Books, 2016], 68).

high and clear air tinged with a "fair elusive beauty,"[2] and over time I grew to love it.

In Narnia I had learned that there was an unseen but real world interwoven with the visible one before me; in Middle-earth, my eyes were opened to its scope. That awakening came at just the right time, there on the cusp of adulthood.

According to Scripture, we live on a vast battlefield. "We do not wrestle against flesh and blood, but against the rulers, against the authorities, against the cosmic powers over this present darkness, against the spiritual forces of evil in the heavenly places" (Eph. 6:12). "Fight the good fight of the faith," Paul enjoins Timothy (1 Tim. 6:12), and elsewhere he writes to the Corinthian church: "Though we walk in the flesh, we are not waging war according to the flesh. For the weapons of our warfare are not of the flesh but have divine power to destroy strongholds" (2 Cor. 10:3–4). When I consider the staggering costs and atrocities of war in our world in the past century alone, this martial imagery underscores the gravity of our situation; its emphasis helps me understand who the real enemy is and what stance I must take in my living.

Yet the awareness of this war is only the beginning of perceiving what is going on around us daily. From time to time, I think about how marvelous and peculiar it is that the Bible ends with a book whose content makes me think of ancient myths. Revelation gives us a sweeping view of the universe in terms we associate with fantasy—dragons and scrolls and armies and wars—when

---

2. J. R. R. Tolkien to Milton Waldman, ca. 1951, in *The Letters of J. R. R. Tolkien,* eds. Humphrey Carpenter and Christopher Tolkien (Boston: Houghton Mifflin, 2000), 144.

it might well have ended, as far as this human's speculation goes, with more epistolary household rules or ecclesiastical guidelines or admonishments to love one another.[3] But the story of our world *is* a story of allegiance and enmity, kingdoms and legions, battles and unexpected courage. And in the midst of the ongoing unseen conflict, there have been those who have steadfastly held places of hope and sanctuary for their people, and those who have valiantly ridden into the heart of the skirmish.

I love, therefore, the Old Testament accounts in which the truth, the stakes, and the reminder of the long war intertwine with the everyday comings and goings of ordinary folk. When Elisha's servant shudders at the sight of Syrian horses and chariots closing in, Elisha prays for his eyes to be opened, assuring him with words that flood me with wonder: "Do not be afraid, for those who are with us are more than those who are with them" (2 Kings 6:16). And the servant sees an overwhelming host of horses and chariots of fire, standing at the ready to protect his master.

The prophet Daniel, though no stranger to visions and conversations with messengers of God, prays a prayer for mercy that brings the angel Gabriel "in swift flight" (Dan. 9:21). Gabriel, in

---

3. "The contribution of the Revelation to the work of witness is not instruction, telling us how to make a coherent apology of the faith, but imagination, strengthening the spirit with images that keep us 'steadfast, immovable, always abounding in the work of the Lord' (1 Cor. 15:58). Instruction in witness is important, but courage is critical, for it takes place in pitched battle. In the work of witness in which we 'fight not against flesh and blood, but against the principalities, against the powers' (Eph. 6:12), we are 'surrounded by so great a cloud of witnesses' (Heb. 12:1). We are among an elect company, well-furnished with heroes" (Eugene H. Peterson, *Reversed Thunder: The Revelation of John and the Praying Imagination* [New York: HarperSanFrancisco, 1988], 112).

fact, reveals that he was sent out with a word before Daniel had even finished his plea, "for you are greatly loved" (Dan. 9:23). Whatever our perception may tell us about our endangerment or our repentant prayers, the reality of our situation is graver and more splendid still.

We live in a story of epic proportions, no matter how easily we forget it. And the same Bible that opens our eyes to this immense reality also gives us plain direction about how its war is to be waged. Our "myth" involves an arsenal of the ordinary: promised prayers earnestly prayed, hidden fasting, secret giving, the continual laying down of our own interests, an open-armed welcome to children, provision for the poor, endurance in trial, and a faithfulness in all these and similar acts, so that when Christ returns, he will find us going about his work. "Our goal is the future of the resurrection—the creation of a new humanity," Keller writes. "And this will come about not with clashing swords but through deeds of sacrificial service, the mark of the upside-down dynamic of cross and resurrection."[4] The "sword" we *are* granted, the singular offensive weapon in the whole of Ephesians 6:11–18, is neither physical instrument nor human tactic; it is the Word of God, about which Eugene Peterson notes, "The warrior Messiah . . . has a single weapon, his word. He wages war by what he *says*, which is an articulation of who he is. . . . We who accompany Jesus across the mountains and through the valleys of salvation are permitted no other weapons."[5]

---

4. Timothy Keller, *Hope in Times of Fear: The Resurrection and the Meaning of Easter* (New York: Viking, 2021), 134.

5. Peterson, *Reversed Thunder,* 164.

In our fight, the artillery of greatest impact is smuggled; the success of our advances depends on the smallest choices. Tolkien knew this well, and wrote of *The Lord of the Rings*:

> [T]he last Tale is to exemplify most clearly a recurrent theme: the place in "world politics" of the unforeseen and unforeseeable acts of will, and deeds of virtue of the apparently small, ungreat, forgotten in the places of the Wise and Great (good as well as evil). A moral of the whole . . . is the obvious one that without the high and noble the simple and vulgar is utterly mean; and without the simple and ordinary the noble and heroic is meaningless.[6]

The same theme runs throughout our world. We have knowledge of what is high, noble, and heroic through the Word of God; we have before us the simple and ungreat means of bringing it to bear in each day of our lives, emphasized by a Lord who commissioned his apostles by stooping to wash their feet.

These, then, are the terms of our war. The King in command has secured the victory and has also laid out the plan of engagement ahead; it is not merely my eternity-drawn eyes that are called to answer but my earthbound feet and hands as well. I am not to forget that the Homeward highway cuts through a battlefield.

---

6. Tolkien to Waldman, *Letters*, 160.

◇ ◇ ◇

These marching orders are fairly straightforward. On my better days I feel like I can take this assignment on and forge ahead with a good will.

In truth, however, I have an Achilles' heel that trips me up far more often than I expect.

The temptation most apt to ambush me isn't a lack of metaphorical weapons or spiritual armor or practical discipline. It's the belief that I am of not much consequence after all and that, if I'm going to attain any kind of significance or make decent headway for the kingdom, I'll have to achieve it or win it through my efforts. As it turns out, that discussion about Éowyn and Arwen was far more telling than it seemed.

In Tolkien's story, Arwen is a kind of lodestar for her people, the elves:

> Young she was and yet not so. . . . the light of stars was in her bright eyes, grey as a cloudless night; yet queenly she looked, and thought and knowledge were in her glance, as of one who has known many things that the years bring. . . . Such loveliness in living thing Frodo had never seen before nor imagined in his mind; and he was both surprised and abashed to find that he had a seat at Elrond's table among all these folk so high and fair.[7]

---

7. J. R. R. Tolkien, *The Lord of the Rings* (Boston: Houghton Mifflin, 1994), 221.

The reverence of the narrating voice and the hobbit-observer stands out to me; in her bearing and attributes, Arwen serves as a source of inspiration during a time of turmoil and war.

But Éowyn is a woman determined to show valor and be remembered *through* battle. She is from a warring nation sandwiched between the advance of evil on one side and of insidious deception on the other. She pleads with Aragorn, the rightful king of Gondor whom she admires and loves, to be allowed to enter into combat beside the horsemen of her land:

> "You are a stern lord and resolute," she said; "and thus do men win renown." She paused. "Lord," she said, "if you must go, then let me ride in your following. For I am weary of skulking in the hills, and wish to face peril and battle. . . . Shall I always be left behind when the Riders depart, to mind the house while they win renown, and find food and beds when they return?"[8]

Éowyn utters the word *renown* three times in their brief conversation, along with "honour" and "victory" and "great deeds." She sees but one means of obtaining these: through "peril" and "battle," to which she longs to "ride" and "wield blade." Thwarted by her duty to govern her people while her uncle the king is away, her strength is channeled into bitterness.

Even after she rides into battle in disguise and deals a death blow to the captain of the enemy's army, she wishes only to leave the Houses of Healing and reenter the fray: "I wish to ride to war like my brother Éomer, or better like Théoden the king, for

---

8. Tolkien, *The Lord of the Rings*, 766–67.

he died and has both honour and peace."[9] Éowyn, "bred among men of war,"[10] desires to make her life count in the only way she knows how.

Her struggle forces me to face my own. As a follower of Christ, I know it is essential to ask myself challenging questions to stay alert and on my feet. Am I being a staunch intercessor? Have I been generous with my time and possessions? Do I exercise trust in difficult seasons? Yet sometimes, especially in the age in which I live, the line between the faithful discharge of duty and the affirmation of renown seems to blur. If no one is moved by my next essay, does that mean it was a waste of time? Where are my credentials—my proof, that is—of a project well received, a child well raised, a spouse happily married? How can I show that I am giving my utmost to my God?

These questions aren't wrong ones to ask, and the answers are nuanced. But one can do all the right things for the wrong reasons—even fighting the good fight. Though it has taken me a long time, I've come to recognize a pattern in my behavior: when I have felt unseen, I've found myself in odd states of mind that lead to feeling aimless and being reckless. I am never more prone to sabotage my life or to do idiotic things than when I believe I am disposable fodder for battle in the kingdom: in marriage, church, friendship circles, artists' groups, anywhere. To this sense of facelessness, renown offers itself as a possible solution: *Earn my company,* it says, *and you'll always feel secure.*

Yet I've spiraled along this cycle long enough to realize that renown isn't really what I want. If I drill down further, a deeper

---

9. Tolkien, *The Lord of the Rings*, 939.

10. Tolkien, *The Lord of the Rings*, 938.

wish lies at the core, one that makes me blush to write openly: a desire to be found beautiful.

I do not mean beautiful in a photogenically remarkable way; I've seen what we humans do to the ones who have that for a time. To be "found beautiful" in my sense means to evoke a response akin to the response beauty has drawn from me; it means to inspire, to brighten, to hold a spot of significance in the heart of another that brings up thoughts of whatever is true, honorable, just, pure, lovely, and so on (Phil. 4:8). It is closely linked, I believe, to what C. S. Lewis spoke of when he addressed our longing for glory: "We do not merely want to *see* beauty, though, God knows, even that is bounty enough. We want something else which can hardly be put into words—to be united with the beauty we see, to pass into it, to receive it into ourselves, to bathe in it, to become part of it."[11] The desire "to become part" of beauty is not an evil or egotistical one in itself. It is a natural want, and to stamp it out would be to deny the way we have been made, the image we bear.

But I cannot win this membership in beauty any more than Éowyn could win a level of renown that would give her peace and hope for the future. From experience, I know that if I make it my primary goal to be found beautiful by people, I will find that human opinion is too ephemeral and human approval too finite to satisfy—besides which, I will find that my own character is too fallible to maintain the admiration of others. There is a way to the wholeness of being known, but it lies through a different gate.

And this is exactly what Éowyn discovers.

---

11. C. S. Lewis, *The Weight of Glory and Other Addresses* (New York: HarperSanFrancisco, 1949), 42.

In the Houses of Healing, a young captain named Faramir perceives that her battle-won renown has not removed her sorrow. With the precision of a doctor extracting poison from a wound, he shows her that even her love for Aragorn was rooted in her drive to matter:

> [H]e was high and puissant, and you wished to
> have renown and glory and to be lifted far above
> the mean things that crawl on the earth. And as
> a great captain may to a young soldier he seemed
> to you admirable. . . . But when he gave you only
> understanding and pity, then you desired to have
> nothing, unless a brave death in battle. Look at
> me, Éowyn![12]

Faramir sees her. He then names her with truth, calling out the courage and nobility of character she has exhibited, in a way only one who loves can. And as Éowyn returns his look "long and steadily," her heart changes, "or else at last she [understands] it."[13] Like a frost-embrittled plain under the soughing of a spring wind, she yields to her healing and says, "[T]he Shadow has departed! I will be a shieldmaiden no longer, nor vie with the great Riders, nor take joy only in the songs of slaying. I will be a healer, and love all things that grow and are not barren."[14]

Éowyn's renouncement is a declaration that she will no longer draw her identity from her role in the fight. It reminds me that all who wait upon Christ, likewise, are not meant to be at war

12. Tolkien, *The Lord of the Rings*, 943.
13. Tolkien, *The Lord of the Rings*, 943.
14. Tolkien, *The Lord of the Rings*, 943.

forever. Called forth by one who knows and loves her, Éowyn finds more within than a soldier and shield-maiden; in their place is a healer, a grower, a cultivator. Faramir acknowledges these new roles with the promise of a place where they can be fulfilled: "I will wed with the White Lady of Rohan, if it be her will. And if she will, then let us cross the River and in happier days let us dwell in fair Ithilien and there make a garden. All things will grow with joy there, if the White Lady comes."[15]

When I look at Éowyn's story, something inside cracks. I remember I have been redeemed—me, not as a tally mark on a salvation sheet but as one sought and seen. From time to time I feel the knowledge of grace come upon me when no one is watching, and the weight of striving and standing firm lifts for a little while. I open to Joy then; I can feel my upturned face soften, and I rejoice in whatever way seems meet. I have sung hushed melodies in dark rooms and danced alone in the kitchen of a sleeping house and lifted autumn-starred eyes to the gloaming sky. I know then with a surety beyond words that I am found beautiful—to him, because of him.

Such moments steady me, and they enable me to lower my defenses while keeping up the armor that counts: to be tender of heart and thick of skin, though that is always hard; to refuse to take myself too seriously; to lay down my life where I am called to, not out of desperation to be seen but out of a knowing compassion. These moments turn me continually from defiance and cynicism to hope and life. In their wake, I often find I am fighting with a clearer heart.

---

15. Tolkien, *The Lord of the Rings*, 943–44.

Some readers object to Éowyn's change, reading submissive relegation to the domestic sphere in the end of her story. But I suggest that her turn is one of the best parts of the book and one that does not diminish her agency as a woman or a warrior. For Tolkien knew as well that we were not made for ceaseless wrestling. Through Éowyn we are given the image of a garden in "fair Ithilien," a reflection of a place prepared for those who will arrive Home spent and scarred, where weary hands will relinquish swords and rejoice to grasp them refashioned as plowshares, where we will no longer be compelled simply to defend life but freed to make it flourish.

Restored and renewed, we will finally enter into the beauty of our King.

Thus the fight continues on a regular July day, right where I am. I turn over a frittata at the stove, pluck bread from the toaster, and call the girls to the table. We read our devotional and I pause, letting eager forks deliver one last quick bite before we begin to pray, and we end with a hymn.

> Be Thou my battle shield, sword for the fight
> Be Thou my dignity, Thou my delight
> Thou my soul's shelter, Thou my high tower
> Raise Thou me heavenward, O Power of my
>   power[16]

---

16. "Be Thou My Vision," attributed to Dallan Forgaill; trans. Mary E. Byrne; versifier Eleanor Hull, 1912.

The words echo trebly in my mind as we sing, renewing a silent prayer that he will always be my dignity, and that I will not try to seek it with my own hand. "You have been my refuge, a strong tower against the enemy" (Ps. 61:3). *Overtake my errant motives. Fix my eyes on you.*

My sight passes over the pans and dishes waiting in the sink, and through invisible movements it cannot apprehend. It surveys the living room and rises to rest over the window on a sign our friends carved, with the name that has come to mean more and more through days like this one.

Ithilien House.

13

Between East and West

Humanly speaking, I owe my existence in part to a bomb.

On June 25, 1950, the North Korean People's Army spilled across the thirty-eighth parallel and invaded the Republic of Korea. Though their people bore a history dating back to the seventh century, these two countries were not yet two years old, having been formed under the influence of the Soviet Union in the north and the United States in the south after World War II.

Not long afterward, my paternal grandfather watched the skies. Then in his mid-thirties, he had been forced to fight in the North Korean army twice and had managed to escape each time by waiting for the air forces of the United Nations Command to drop their bombs. During the explosions, he and other coercively recruited men scattered and fled. He returned home to his wife and four young children, but was brought back.

The third time, he knew he had no other choice; if anything was going to change, he would have to escape on his own first.

He managed to make his way south and became an ammunition carrier for the U.S. military.

Meanwhile, his family was placed under close watch in the Communist village leader's house for a year. When they were released, my grandmother took the children and headed to a village near the Yellow Sea. There she joined the support network for the resistance fighters who came by needing food and aid. North Korean soldiers knew of the system and visited the village, posing as the resistance in order to catch the residents in the act, but Grandmother quickly learned how to spot the pretenders. They didn't know the subtle signals, such as a double-stamp of feet outside the door. "You could simply tell who they were," she later said, "from their words and actions."

After a time, a message came for my grandmother: the resistance had found a way to get her and her children out of the North. They were to come down to the shoreline to meet the boat at a certain time of the night. When the appointed hour came, they left: the three older children and my grandmother on foot, with the youngest on my grandmother's back.

They would have to cross a creek on their way to the sea. Knowing what was at stake for each life, she soberly told the older children to hold hands and walk together, adding a word of caution that has never been forgotten and rends my own mother-heart today: "If one of you is swept off your feet by the current and dragged away to drown, don't make a sound."

Fortunately, all five of them arrived safely to the shore and hid in the reeds. At a signal from the guerrilla fighter there, they boarded the boat, which took them to a safe island not far away. Eventually they made their way to Daecheongdo, whose name means "Large Blue Island." My grandmother had heard that Grandfather was living there, assisting the local fishermen. Though Daecheongdo is only 4.3 miles long and less than 4 miles wide,[1] its beaches and roads would prove to be a wonderland for the children. The island still belongs to South Korea today, in a position along the demarcation line that startles me every time I look it up. The reunited family made a home there in a small thatched house, on a plot of land where they raised trees for firewood. Three more children were born to them after the war ended; one of them was my father.

Meanwhile, 114 miles to the southeast, my maternal grandfather and grandmother—my Halmoni and Haraboji[2]—had made their home in one of the houses belonging to my great-grandfather, a law professor. Great-grandfather had a long "Kaiser Wilhelm" mustache and beard, large eyes, a narrow nose, and extensive landholdings in Seonsan, Seoul, and Kunpo that he inherited from his father. The records of his clan were dotted with government ministers and men who placed great value on the education of their children. In those days, it was said, you could walk forty *ri* (about twelve miles) from one end of the Seonsan property to the other.

When the North Korean army pushed the war front down the peninsula in July 1950 and evacuation orders were issued, Halmoni and Haraboji took their three-month-old son and left

---

1. Neighboring Socheongdo ("Small Blue Island") is smaller; about 3 miles long and 1.86 miles wide.

2. For the reader's ease, I've used the Korean words for "grandmother" and "grandfather" here to refer to my maternal grandparents.

with six other relatives. After walking for more than half a day, they arrived on the banks of Nakdong River.

The bridges had been destroyed. They made a plan to cross the water on a raft under the cover of darkness. The raft kept sinking, however, and the baby was hungry, so they decided instead to ford the river at dawn. The water wasn't too deep; Haraboji found that if he stood straight up, he could keep his face out of the water. So with the baby on his shoulders and my Halmoni holding onto him, they crossed, bobbing up and descending with each step.

Halmoni was so preoccupied by her fear that they might be spotted by North Korean soldiers that she could barely keep track of their progress. But as they neared the opposite bank, she saw a strange sight: heads popping up along the ground, as if the bodies they belonged to had been buried up to their necks. When the family finally emerged from the river, a dozen South Korean soldiers came out of a trench to greet them and hold the baby. "Welcome," they said, warmly. "Well done."

Later that day, the family arrived in downtown Daegu and found two rentals near the hospital, which they paid for by selling Halmoni's and Haraboji's cousin's wedding rings. They gave the remaining money to a distant relative, asking him to buy a sack of rice and a sack of barley for their stay, but the relative took the money and disappeared. Suddenly left with no means to buy food, the cousin suggested that she and Halmoni grow bean sprouts to sell at the local market. Thankfully the plan worked, and for three months they lived as refugees in the city, holding the baby's one-hundred-day celebration there as well.

The evacuation order was lifted in the winter of 1950, and Halmoni, Haraboji, and their baby son returned to the Seonsan house. Eventually they moved to Seoul. But they visited Daegu often after Great-grandfather and Great-grandmother moved there, and on one such visit, my mother was born.

These stories are a part of me, passed down through conversations, embedded habits, and traditions.

But in 1995, as the plane touches down on the runway at Gimpo Airport, I am not aware of any of these stories of turmoil and fear, of courage and sheer survival, that have come before me on this very soil.

Instead, my first views of South Korea come sideways as I rest my motion-sick head on my mother's knee in the car. Countless cousins and uncles and aunts, it seems, have come to welcome us into their homes in Incheon before we make our way to Seoul; a caravan of cars moves between square-shaped little trucks and gray taxis along the winding roads. A statue of a huge ship with waving sailors, topped by an arch with a woman stretching her arms upward to the heavens, glides by the window. As we get out of the car, I catch a tinge of salt upon the air and ask my parents, "Are we near the ocean?"

Fielding a dozen questions from our relatives, they nod. I look around to see if I can spot it somewhere in the distance and find it with the help of an older cousin—between the gray high-rise apartment buildings, the steely line of a northern sea.

◇ ◇ ◇

Sooner than I expect, I carve a welcome groove of familiarity through my new surroundings. Explorations in food help. My favorite among the ice cream treats at the grocer's, I decide, is the

Double Bianco—vanilla ice cream swirled with strawberry syrup, with a layer of apple sorbet in the bottom for a tart finish. The flavors go well together, but I'm most taken with the tiny spoon that comes in its own notched compartment. During the hour-long commute to school via bus and subway and walking, I trot beside my father and watch the seasons reflected in the street-side food carts: flat *ppopgi* lollipops in the summer, made from melted sugar and baking soda in the tiniest pans over an open flame; toasted red-bean-paste-filled pastries and *hodo gwaja*—spherical walnut cookies—under the ginkgo trees in autumn; in winter, spicy *tteok kkochi* rice cake skewers and savory fishcakes steaming in pans of soothing broth.

Outside the church I attend, I regularly stop to purchase *hotteok* from a deaf husband and wife who cook them in a mesmerizing iron device. Deftly she rolls dough in her hands while he mixes the brown sugar filling, and in a trice flattened circles land in a double row of circular molds. The wife claps each mold shut, like a domino cascade of small slamming doors, and when the heat underneath cooks the bottom, she uses a small metal hook to quickly flip each closed circle around. She never misses. The result is a stack of light, hollow pancakes with a touch of syrup lacing the insides, perfectly chewy around the edges and crispy enough to snap into pieces at their thin middles.

"Two?" she mouths, holding her gloved fingers up to me, and I shake my head and motion back, relieved that I don't have to run the gauntlet of small talk.

"Just one, please."

Eventually I learn to navigate public transportation in addition to food orders, though always with a measure of trepidation.

When do I need to pull the cord for my bus stop? Will I get tongue-tied buying my subway ticket today? Do I have the right amount of change? One afternoon a taxi driver loses his temper with my soft and haltingly spoken words. He mutters an epithet for the mentally challenged, loud enough to reach my ear, as I get out of the car.

For an introverted girl in middle school who hates being singled out for negative reasons, public admonishment is the highest mark of shame. Yet there seem to be so many hapless ways to achieve it: setting foot on grass anywhere in the city, failing to keep my balance as the bus lurches over steep streets, being young in a culture of numerous hierarchies. Over and over again, I feel small. And I am.

I watch the unguarded conduct of the country from my height, the way a passerby in a store winces at a parent losing patience with a child or a foreigner picks up the slang of a new tongue before its poetry. "Speak Korean!" an elderly man snaps on an afternoon train, nearly spitting his words out. He steps toward the spot where I stand talking with my friends and teacher. "This is Korea, eh? In Korea you speak Korean!" We can smell the alcohol on his breath. Our international school does not allow its students to speak Korean when we are in the building, but in the outside world we encounter strangers who demand that we speak no other language.

The man's tirade underscores a disorienting fact: here I can blend in if I don't open my mouth. I no longer stand out as one of two East Asian students in my grade at Hardin Park Elementary, where I had to constantly explain that Korea wasn't a part of China or Japan; I am no longer instantly identifiable as a minority. It is jarringly easy to fade into the background. I've become what Marilyn Gardner calls an "invisible immigrant,"[3] and my vantage point feels like the kind that is buried deep in the folds of a family instead of one that belongs to a guest.

Age-based hierarchical bullying is everywhere. I escape much of it at school because my behavior and background are too American, but even so, I am occasionally taken to task for inadvertently disrespecting an older student. All the younger students, including me, vow to treat our schoolmates better as we advance through the grade levels, but power can be funny; we notice the irony that once it's in hand, the system doesn't seem so broken.

Materialism and an obsession with appearance pervade my surroundings as well. I am made to understand that brand names on purses and backpacks matter. So do double eyelids, which are easily obtainable through plastic surgery; a proper bust-waist-hip ratio; pale skin; thinner noses; sharp jawlines. The pressure to look acceptable is as heavy as the pressure to perform well in school and at work. When my mother and I come back to our apartment building at ten one night after running errands, we run into our neighbor, who is taking her son to his next tutoring session at a *hakwon*. He'll study until past midnight, come home, sleep, go to school in the morning, and repeat the cycle, like the rest of his peers.

With the evidence of these burdens around me, the drinking culture ceases to be surprising. Evening news reports become

---

3. "*Invisible Immigrant.* Understanding the migrant experience to another country yet being seen outwardly as one who is originally from that country; that sense of having much in common with the immigrant experience and yet looking so much like those around us that we are assumed to be one of the crowd. Our immigrant sensibilities are invisible" (Marilyn Gardner, *Worlds Apart* [n.p.: Doorlight, 2018], 189).

decipherable, and I listen wide-eyed to pithy accounts about men and women who have jumped from tall buildings to escape poverty or ostracization or societal shame.

To be sure, no one is unaware of these negative traits of Korean society; TV shows, comedy sketches, and interviews frequently point them out. They seem especially strange to me only because I am fresh from a different culture with its own shortcomings and besetting sins.

Some days, spent by all the contrasts, I retreat. I take a book from my backpack and read it on the subway, though I know the English-language cover will attract the friendly envy of mothers and the hand-smothered whispers of uniformed schoolgirls—not to mention the occasional barrage of verbal shrapnel. I need the refuge and the comfort I find through these portals to other places and other lives.

While the dozing heads of strangers nod onto my shoulder and waves of commuters come and go, I immerse myself in historical fiction, young adult paperbacks, discipleship books, and biographies. Amy Carmichael. Corrie ten Boom. Jim and Elisabeth Elliot. Hudson Taylor. George Müller. John and Betty Stam. Seoul fades; Dohnavur, Haarlem, and Bristol beckon in its place. I thirst for stories about men and women who wholeheartedly believed the Word of God, and as I read, the land and culture around me seem to grow less and less relevant to my newfound faith.

The story that matters is the story of the Fall and of Christ's death and resurrection, after all. I see it played out over and over in a thousand different contexts with bravery, sacrifice, creativity, and love. Page by page, I'm reminded that I do not have to tie my identity to the question posed by every relative and stranger who demands to know which home I like more, "Korea or America?" As a child of Abraham by faith (Rom. 4), I tell myself, the truest heritage I hold is rooted in a new covenant and a better country.

When I move back to the States after eleventh grade, an inward part of me braces myself for another sea change, consoled in part to know that I won't have to constantly run up against the limits of language.

I shake the dust of my growing-up years from my heels and, along with it, the bulk of my experience of an entire country.

◇ ◇ ◇

In the summer of 2018, a book of photographs of Korea lies innocently on the coffee table. On my way through the room between chores, I walk around it, eyeing it without opening it. I've borrowed it from the library because my daughters want to learn more about the language and culture of their heritage, but I am not sure where to begin their introduction.

During an afternoon break I turn its pages, following long-forgotten features on glossy pages with my fingertips. Rocks emerge from thickly forested mountains like the chipped bark of giant trees rising up through moss in an ancient fairy tale. Traditional *hanok* tile roofs curve upward at their corners, reflecting the rise and fall of surrounding landscapes. Schoolchildren grin over tantalizing snacks from street vendors, while men and women in tailored suits hurry to work between skyscrapers and monks traverse garden paths between hundred-year-old trees. I linger over these images, as if looking at them hard enough will expand their frames.

They suggest to me that more is stored in my memory than I have cared to recall.

As if they have been waiting for this reintroduction, other prompts appear from surprising quarters. Our neighbors ask us for translation help when they host members of a visiting tae kwon do team and are shocked that I speak the language better than I have apparently let on. One friend gifts me a translated copy of *The Hen Who Dreamed She Could Fly,* which leaves me raw but reflective; another friend passes me the name of a Korean drama series, *Crash Landing on You,* that sets both laughter and bittersweet contemplation mingling in the air around Yongwon and me for weeks. Meanwhile, a guild colleague sends links to the YouTube channels of Korean homesteaders whom she finds calming and inspiring—and these, besides reminding me of the sparkling cleaning standards of my mother, teach me new ways to pay attention to the sizzle of food and the sound of a good rainstorm. Even the man who comes to clean our air ducts launches into a rhapsody about how much he loves *soondubu jjigae,* a spicy soft tofu stew, when he learns that we are Korean. "Man," he exclaims, on his way out the door, "now I'm going to have to pick some up on the way home!" None of these people, save one, are Korean themselves.

I listen to all their recommendations, mostly because they do not come from people who are telling me they appreciate diversity or my fascinating foreign background; they are from people who are calling me to share in the specifics of something notable they've experienced from a culture I know—or thought I knew. Their enthusiasm makes me willing to reenter the world I left behind.

And slowly I remember.

Relatives who enfolded us on holidays, talking late into the night, aunts and cousins forever urging another bite from loaded tables. Endless curiosities to peruse with friends in Paris Baguette bakeries and stationery stores. A kind manager at the Word of Life bookstore near Gwanghwamun Station who recognized me even when years passed between my visits and who always pressed a small gift into my astonished hand when I left. The university and graduate students who came to my father's office to ask him for life advice. Street dancers who directed traffic outside parking garages with a dozen unnecessary but fluidly captivating motions. The atmosphere of living in a society where the people address friends and schoolmates with familial nicknames like *oppa* (older brother, to a female speaker), *hyung* (older brother to a male), *unni* (older sister to a female), and *nuna* (older sister to a male).

I think of the deference people were always expected to show to older generations, and the values my mom and dad tried to instill in me about being generous, dependable, and acting with honor. I begin to ask my parents questions about their own parents and grandparents. As they reminisce, I discover favorite details from the feast of history they spread before me.

Grandfather was prone to seasickness, for instance, and could not make a living as a fisherman on that small island, so the family raised vegetables and melons instead.

In his free time as a young boy, my dad would sometimes catch a string of fish or gather abalones and bring them home to his mother, and beam with happiness at her thanks for contributing to the family's provisions.

Around the same time, in my mother's world, Haraboji passed away at age forty-four. Mom sensed that she would have to be responsible to look after herself and do well in her schooling from then on. But she was too far into the school year to catch up one lesson at a time, so she memorized her textbooks from cover to cover to get by until she could study more thoroughly.

Stirred up by these recovered memories and stories, my impressions of my ancestral land return anew, and a hidden chest of emotion cracks open. How can I describe the intimations of wholeness I see as I look back and hear echoes of a hundred songs and walk old routes in my mind? There is a particular kind of gravitas in Korea and its people—an innate familiarity with the grief of separation, a sorrowful hope mixed with ready humor, and a nuance and a poignancy I want to pass on in the way I tell my own stories. I hope these threads endure in me. I wish I had had the eyes to see them more clearly when I was a child.

But I find deep consolation in the fact that the Creator of this universe knows all the traits of the people groups he created. He holds their stories. He knows the name of every family that was torn in two when the Korean War ended and the peninsula was divided in half; he knows who among my relatives I will meet for the first time in eternity. All the unrecorded details I wonder about in the Bible, all the family tales I have never heard—he remembers them all, and thousands more besides.

In part, the kingdom of God and its members have been responsible for honing my sight to recognize the sacrifice, creativity, and love in my heritage. And this is fitting, for the kingdom as it shall be will encompass cultures and the identities that make them uniquely beautiful *without* homogenizing them. We are told "the nations will walk by [the light of the glory of God and the Lamb], and the kings of the earth will bring their glory into it.

The city's gates shall stand open day after day—and there will be no night there. Into the city they will bring the splendours and honours of the nations" (Rev. 21:24–26 PHILLIPS). Keller delves into the striking picture of this promise:

> These visions of the final age show that our racial and cultural distinctions are part of God's good creation and so important that they will be carried over into the new creation, not eradicated but purified of all the sinful distortions, just as our bodies with their distinctions will be brought in and purified of all weakness and decay. The people of God in the new world will not be homogenous but will consist of "every nation, tribe, people and language" (Rev. 7:9). They will be *a single* people (Rev. 5:9) still marked by these differences. Yet these differences will only make our unity greater and the new humanity more beautiful in all its glory.[4, 5]

---

4. Timothy Keller, *Hope in Times of Fear: The Resurrection and the Meaning of Easter* (New York: Viking, 2021), 138.

5. Bavinck shares similar thoughts: "But in the new heaven and new earth the world as such is restored; in the believing community the human race is saved. In that community, which Christ has purchased and gathered from all nations, languages, and tongues (Rev. 5:9, etc.), all the nations, Israel included, maintain their distinct place and calling (Matt. 8:11; Rom. 11:25; Rev. 21:24; 22:2). And all those nations—each in accordance with its own distinct national character—bring into the new Jerusalem all they have received from God in the way of glory and honor (Rev. 21:24, 26)" (Herman Bavinck, *The Last Things: Hope for This World and the Next,* ed. John Bolt, trans. John Vriend [Grand Rapids: Baker Books, 1996], 160).

There shall be, then, aspects of the New Jerusalem that are distinctly Korean, American, Japanese, Haitian, Ecuadorian, and Armenian, among many others. When I think of the suffering, the art, the music, the hope, the pain, the customs, the flavors, and the tastes that have shaped each people group into what it is, the "splendors of the nations" seems to me a matchless and apt phrase.

Meanwhile, although I've often felt like I am on the fringes of the cultures I have lived in and loved, I'm starting to understand that this intersecting space is an excellent spot to look forward to those splendors that are to be revealed. The thread of Homeward longing has led me even into the past, with its troubling and triumphant stories branching in every direction, and the Word at the center of the universe, who was with God and was God and was in the beginning with God (John 1:1–2), is the word of redemption that makes sense of all of them.

Someday, according to this Word, "people will come from east and west, and from north and south, and recline at table in the kingdom of God" (Luke 13:29). Ah, I believe the stories shared there will be an unparalleled exhibition of glory as we piece together the majesty and the vast, wild wisdom of his plan.

For now, I still carry disconnected life chapters with me. Some resonate with people where I live now, some make better sense on the other side of the planet, and some are familiar only to those who know what it's like to be caught in between worlds.

The stories in my bloodline carry a testimony to the sundering power of water. Always, it seems, the act of crossing undertows and tides has meant going into unknown territory while stifling retrospection and fear.

But according to sacred rumor, "there is a river whose streams make glad the city of God, the holy habitation of the Most High" (Ps. 46:4). The image John gives from his vision gives me hope: "Then the angel showed me the river of the water of life, bright as crystal, flowing from the throne of God and of the Lamb through the middle of the street of the city; also, on either side of the river, the tree of life with its twelve kinds of fruit, yielding its fruit each month. The leaves of the tree were for the healing of the nations" (Rev. 22:1–2). This river will water the city where the nations bring their honors, giving life instead of threatening it, offering healing on both its sides.

It is a river that extends a particular welcome, I believe, to all who have ever felt split by their backgrounds. At its banks, whole at last, we will share and listen and celebrate; we will never need to leave anything behind.

No matter where or how many times we cross those waters, we will be Home.

14

On Beauty in Creation

It is an extravagance, and I know it.

I passed by this small journal in one of my favorite bookshops for months, stopping to admire it a few times, but I always ended up placing it back on the rack. I couldn't think of a use for it that would justify the purchase.

Yet there was something about the illuminated, intertwined borders and the gaiety of color that continued to pique my interest; I liked the neatly bound feel of the gilded spine in the hand and the compact concentration of the bright garden on its cover. I spotted the emerald book in various sizes in other bookstores and stationery shops, but I liked the miniature version best.

I can't remember where I was on the day I finally bought it—can't recall if it was a gleam of loveliness in a hope-hungry day, or if I took up the jewel-toned book to commemorate a family excursion in the golden days of summer. I do know that it has lain long on my desk as I've tried to figure out its purpose; it hasn't seemed right, somehow, to make it a repository for random scribbles.

But today I know what it should be.

I unfasten the little brass clasp and turn to the front page. Slowly I pen the title, willing my hand not to make any rogue marks: *A Book of Beauties displaying the nearness, grace, and love of God, and of Springlike Hopes.*

The words are a planting of a flag.

Although I grew up valuing the lovely features in my surroundings, once I became a Christian in the mid-1990s, I became cautious about placing a premium on beauty. For a semester in college, I led a no-frills Bible study with no refreshments and little social time for its members; our small leaders' team of three earnestly wanted Scripture to be the main feature and attraction of our gathering. At best, in those days, beauty felt like a luxurious "extra"; at worst, it held the potential to be a distraction from a single-minded focus on Christ.

My perspective softened after college, but it was only when a series of debilitating panic attacks struck a few years ago that I finally looked my asceticism full in the face. "The breakdown," as I've come to call it, was a culmination of many events; it was set off by a fuse of fear that had thickened and coiled through the years, threading through circumstances where I felt both responsible and powerless.

More important than the cause, however, is where the following months forced me to go; they plunged me into an examination of my faith in the goodness of God. What kind of events might he bring about in my life that I would have to brace myself for? What did it mean for him to be sovereign and omniscient in a world of suffering?

Peeling back layers of hitherto unspoken questions, I uncovered a denser fear at their center: I was afraid some great crisis would happen and I would "know" cerebrally that God is "good," but no longer be able to see him or comprehend his goodness under the burden of an unbearable grief or pain. I have scrambled to hide knives from others who were bent on self-harm; I've stood in too-small rooms watching old friendships detonate in the space of a second. I have held the limp body of a sick child. I could no longer see what might keep me from shattering with the next sudden event.

I became desperate to know whether he was truly near.

Through those long months, I walked about learning how to inhale and exhale, how to rest without breaking into a constant sweat. I sang hymns quietly to manage my breathing because my mind seemed to have forgotten the rhythm, and when it all became too much, I would retreat to the garden and let the tears fall without speech. "Help me" became a regular prayer under my breath, from putting my socks on in the morning to trying to wind down for sleep at night. It was not an intentionally instituted practice. The two words were a real-time request, made in the knowledge that if my Father did not show up, there would simply be no help for me. I told him as much.

And slowly, between these petitions, small sights here and there caught my eye. A sunset of golden fleece unrolled itself across the broad horizon outside the thrift store. A speckle-breasted, fledgling robin tried its wings out in the garden and fluttered clumsily up to the fence. In their wake I felt a startling shot of wonder and followed a subdued chain of thought that built, link by link, upon itself:

> *If I had been two minutes late, I wouldn't have caught this sight.*
>
> *If God knows everything, I suppose he knows right now where I will be at any given time.*
>
> *Perhaps he put me right at this spot, then, at this minute, on purpose.*
>
> *Maybe it's worth keeping watch for the next thing.*

Thus, when I could not keep in mind the long view of living Homeward—or any long view at all—and I asked for help, he showed up through daily coruscations of beauty, especially in natural creation. Each one was a reminder of his disposition and his love. Each one taught me, at a critical juncture, to take beauty personally, to receive its existence and its instances as a line of live communication from my Lord.

"Consider the ravens" (Luke 12:24), Jesus said, while he was here. "Consider the lilies" (v. 27). He told us to look at the birds and the wildflowers not merely as an analogy or metaphor but as a plain demonstration of the character of God. That demonstration is right before us, in short, and he has placed it there for us if we have the eyes to see it. Psalm 147 details his acts in both human civilization and nature, giving a picture of the commingling of his closeness and his sovereignty.

In Montgomery's *Rilla of Ingleside,* a teacher ponders God's view of World War I and wonders aloud if "the Power that runs the universe" thinks of the war as lightly as humans regard an anthill being destroyed. John Meredith, a minister, counters this statement instantly: "You forget . . . that an infinite Power must be infinitely little as well as infinitely great. We are neither, therefore there are things too little as well as too great for us to apprehend. To the infinitely little an ant is of as much importance as a mastodon."[1] As easy as it is for us to feel lost amid the buckling spasms of relational crises, political movements, and inadequate social systems, Jesus states clearly that the littlest and most overlooked are watched over constantly by our Father (Matt. 18:10). "Are not two sparrows sold for a penny? And not one of them will fall to the ground apart from your Father. But even the hairs of your head are all numbered. Fear not, therefore; you are of more value than many sparrows" (Matt. 10:29–31). The ant, the sparrow, even the fear-shackled woman struggling to make it through the day—each one is under the care of a Creator who is "gracious and merciful, slow to anger and abounding in steadfast love" (Ps. 145:8). I had long known that "his invisible attributes, namely, his eternal power and divine nature, have been clearly perceived, ever since the creation of the world, in the things that have been made" (Rom. 1:20), but it had not truly come home to me that such care for the unremarkable and the helpless was part of that divine nature.

The idea that the details of beauty placed around me were gifts, then, and not mere happenstance, made me begin to take notice of my environment—the way a stack of mail suddenly grows interesting when one spots one's address spelled out in handwritten script. Each surprise, each sun-shower falling diagonally to highlight the hundred shadowy ridges of the Rocky

---

1. L. M. Montgomery, *Rilla of Ingleside* (London: Puffin, 1993), 195.

Mountains, each unforeseen salutation from a friend taught me over and over again that God is a God of eucatastrophe:[2] a wild-card God whose specific actions I could not predict but whose character I could rely upon in whatever the future might bring. I had somehow grown accustomed to anticipating the worst without factoring in his presence. Because I could not imagine what he might do, in my projections I cut him out of the picture entirely. But what the finch songs, windstorms, and dew-spangled blades of grass showed me was that he was capable of showing up anywhere. Every parcel of beauty, magnifying the testimony of Scripture, was telling me that I could expect a goodness that I would recognize as good.

My response, unforced and nearly unnoticed for a time, rose as worship. His beauty was constant enough, bright and startling enough, to bring forth singing in the shadow of his wings.

And it has brought me here. I flip to a fresh page, make my first entry, and begin the practice of jotting down what I see: blackberries in Greek yogurt, a neighbor bringing dry ice over to create fog for the girls for fun, a shared flash of anticipation with my husband about meeting again after we part on this earth, snow crystals lacing the top of the scalloped fence.

Seven months after beginning the little journal, I sum up its purpose for friends.

This, then, is my small book of beauties: my offering of gratitude for the

---

2. *Eucatastrophe* is a term coined by Tolkien to describe "the good catastrophe, the sudden joyous 'turn'" in a story that "denies . . . universal final defeat" (J. R. R. Tolkien, "On Fairy-Stories," in *Tree and Leaf,* rev. ed. [London: HarperCollins, 2001], 68–69).

constant newness of his mercies, which are often as fresh and unexpected as snowdrops springing from the lately frozen earth; my attempt to be attentive to the beauties that, like grace notes upon a melody, speak volumes about the Composer of this world. It is my (insufficient) record of the kind of love he has for us, evidenced through Christ and rippling out in a thousand vivifying waves from the Resurrection—a love unaccountably brazen, sacrificial, refining, noble, and ennobling.

An extravagance.

◇ ◇ ◇

October 23, 2019

Her small hand is smeared pewter gray from her drawing, a graphite stamp leaving smudges on the tabletop and on her paper. But it is one of the loveliest things in the world, I think—this hand belonging to a tiny artist who recognizes that one of the most powerful ways she can show love to others is through the writing of notes and the drawing of pictures.

November 16, 2019

A few days ago, over our reading of our current book, I paused for a moment to animatedly share a thought with our older daughter. The way she turned toward me to listen startled me: eyebrows raised, mirth and interest and sympathy in the expression of her eyes—a sudden portrait of both the gracious woman she will one day be, and, even now, the nine-year-old who could have approached that conversation with a bored air, and didn't.

May 22, 2021

Awoke this morning to repetitive squawks and opened the window blearily to see a standoff between a scolding magpie in the elm tree and a

squirrel on the fence with a peanut in its mouth. Thankfully my motion of
folding the blinds startled the magpie into retreating to a nearby roof. The
squirrel passed, and the noise stopped.

   Early morning squabbles notwithstanding, how I love this season, and
the first flush of new green on the trees, and the tulips, and the nodding blue
flax, and the waking promise in everything.

As I add to the book, the entries remind me that "God cannot give what He hasn't got—He cannot produce what He does
not possess," as Norman Geisler says. "Therefore," Geisler continues, "God is beautiful; His creation is merely a reflection of His
beauty. All beauty comes from God; hence, all beauty is like God.
All who create beauty imitate God."[3] When we witness beauty, we
are witnessing him.

But the entries remind me, too, that even a sharp eye for
beauty is not a panacea for the ills and evils of the world—not
on its own. It will not take away grief. It does not abolish pain.
It does not guard against tragedy, and it does not resolve all-too-
legitimate causes of fear.

Beauty itself, moreover, can be manipulated to mislead and
distort our perception of truth. From the sirens of Homer's *Odyssey*
to the book of Proverbs' injunction that "charm is deceitful, and
beauty is vain" (31:30), the ancient world was aware of the captivating power of beauty and the ways in which such power could
be wielded for deceptive ends. That knowledge has not faded
over time. George MacDonald's *The Princess and Curdie*, published in 1883, unfolds one of the most horrific scenes I have

---

3. Norman L. Geisler, *Systematic Theology: In One Volume* (Minneapolis:
Bethany House, 2002), 527.

ever encountered—not because of any particular gruesomeness on MacDonald's part, but because of how thoroughly it subverts my instincts.

Curdie, a young boy on a journey, stops in the middle of an unfamiliar heath to take rest under the only tree for miles. Soon he hears a gorgeous song that seems to be winging its way to him, and indeed, as the music draws nearer, he sees that it is being sung by a flock of large birds. They gather around him and begin an entrancing dance, thwarted a little by the presence of a large and hideous animal named Lina who has been instructed to attend Curdie. The dance and the hauntingly sweet song lull Curdie into a drowsy state, and right as he is falling asleep, he wakes up in excruciating pain: "The birds were upon him—all over him—and had begun to tear him with beaks and claws."[4] He is only saved because the repulsive creature who is with him attacks the birds and takes the brunt of their ire, and MacDonald concludes the scene by stating clearly, "Lina was no beauty certainly, but already, the first night, she had saved his life."[5]

The strangeness of perverted or hollow beauty feels inherently wrong, like a lovely face devoid of compassion or humanity, or the cold touch of terrible news on a bright summer day. It feels wrong because beauty was never meant to be unnaturally singled out and isolated. But when beauty is united with truth and goodness, when she is a servant and not a mistress of what we know to be real, she becomes a blessed usher. Thus restored, every beauty

---

4. George MacDonald, *The Princess and Curdie* (London: Puffin, 1966), 93.

5. MacDonald, *The Princess and Curdie*, 94.

tells us more about its Cause and Source; it works in concert with truth to ground us back in his great goodness.

So I have come to receive beauty in creation—in the garden, in nature, in people—as manna on the Homeward road.[6] It is a daily provision, a traveler's bread that tells me Joy comes from a far more able and generous hand than my own, and that there will be more tomorrow. As I choose to receive these sustaining portions, they are keeping my heart soft and my vision trained to recognize the true character of my God.

Along the way, I am realizing that I have not loved the world overmuch. I have not loved it enough for what it *is*. A balance must always be struck between learning to receive earthly beauties and not letting them impede our longing for their Origin, but on the whole I'd rather have what the poet Tom Andrews called "Attention Surplus Disorder"[7] than skew towards soul blindness—so that the beauty I see fuels my hunger and trains my palate for the beauty that is to come.

◇ ◇ ◇

The still evening hours of the summer half-light bring the most beautiful moments in the year to our house. Yongwon

---

6. I've since discovered that I am not the only one to regard beauty in this way. Tish Harrison Warren writes: "The old saying is true: hunger is the best condiment. As I endured the mystery of loss, any picture of beauty, moral or physical, was like manna" (Tish Harrison Warren, *Prayer in the Night* [Downers Grove, IL: InterVarsity Press, 2021], 62).

7. Tom Andrews, "North of the Future," in *Random Symmetries* (Oberlin, OH: Oberlin College Press, 2002), 264. Anthony Doerr beautifully demonstrates the richness of living out this "disorder" in his memoir *Four Seasons in Rome*.

knows where to find me—and sometimes where to send me—in this lucent window of time right before and after the sun slips below the serrated mountain line. If there weren't dinner dishes to fill and bedtime stories to read, I would likely be in my reading chair from golden hour through twilight with my chin on my knees, watching the Redeemer of all things transform sky and silhouette into wonders unimaginable at midday.

Here, for reasons I do not care to investigate, I steep in the peace that "surpasses all understanding" (Phil. 4:7) and note the effect of his presence: my own rush-riddled soul, calmed and quieted, unfurled, released into the humility of knowing no rescue or merit but his. Abiding in his sustenance, I am gentled—and strengthened—and made inexpressibly jubilant.

According to 1 Corinthians 13, keeping a "record of wrongs" (v. 5 NIV) goes against the nature of love. I think I am finding that the inverse is also true. Keeping a record of the constant flow of beauties I encounter, in all their detail and flavor and color, is an experience of reading a love so immoderate that the life it nourishes cannot help but overflow.

I know there is a good chance these words will look pale and otherworldly under tomorrow's workaday gaze. But tonight I glance up at a live tree trunk glowing in the last embers of sunlight and feel that creation is often surer and clearer in its knowledge of the coming glories than I am. It is no idle act to watch it sing its prelude to freedom, and know that the Creator for whom it sings is here.

15

At the Ends of the Imagination

My younger daughter climbs onto my chair and turns around to peer at the calendar print on the wall behind my desk. It is Wednesday afternoon, and time for our weekly tea date. I set up the tray table in our usual corner and head to the kitchen to fill a little china teacup with milk and tuck two checkerboard cookies onto the saucer.

When I return, to my surprise, she is still studying the art.

The print is a square reproduction of Alan Lee's rendering of the Grey Havens from *The Return of the King,* framed in a band of silver and blue. She hasn't read any of Tolkien's work yet—I am saving the stories until she's a little older—but it seems that some-thing in the scene has sparked her imagination. Knowing that I won't give her any definitive answers beyond a smile and a cheery "maybe" to her questions, she muses aloud in a long stream.

"These look like aqueducts. I see three people standing there in the middle. That thing on the end looks like the three-legged thing that holds up the camera; what do you call it?

"The statue in the middle looks like somebody dressed it. Just that one.

"There's a ship. I think someone's sailing away, Mommy. . . . I wonder who it is and where they're going."

At these last words my heart catches. I coax her over and we have our read-aloud and conversation time, but after she leaves and the westering sun casts a thin amber veil over the print, my thoughts turn toward the signposts of Homeward longing that have meant a great deal to me, like this one.

What in this scene persists in arresting my attention? As far as Middle-earth settings go, many value Rivendell, that "perfect house, whether you like food or sleep, or story-telling or singing, or just sitting and thinking best, or a pleasant mixture of them all,"[1] the Elven sanctuary that serves as "a cure for weariness, fear, and sadness."[2] Yet to me the harbor of the Grey Havens is far more poignant, and of all literary locations, this is the one I wanted to have where I could walk by it regularly. Every time I revisit this scene, my heart leaves with Frodo right out of the port. The slanted sail, the glad passenger, the prow pointed toward the horizon, the promise of "white shores and beyond them a far green country under a swift sunrise":[3] all these together move me to a sweet and sad relief beyond words.

The Grey Havens is a site of departure, not arrival, and as such it is emblematic for me of the realities that lie beyond this life, of which we are given hints but no extensive details. It reminds me

---

1. J. R. R. Tolkien, *The Lord of the Rings* (Boston: Houghton Mifflin, 1994), 219.
2. Tolkien, *The Lord of the Rings*, 219.
3. Tolkien, *The Lord of the Rings*, 1007.

that amid all the conjectures we might cherish about the life to come, we have mostly approximations; the rest is mystery. But the Grey Havens is not the only subject that regularly invites me into Homeward longing. Through the years I've been grateful to recognize the pattern of other motifs and elements scattered throughout my life and the lives of others.

◇ ◇ ◇

In the ocean I hear a voice that intimates great depths and great constancy, and I cannot specify exactly what draws me to its sight and sound more with each year that passes. But J. B. Phillips offers some insight: "To be beside the sea is not only to provide a breath of fresh air for the body but a draught of peace for the mind, a reminder that the feverish activity of human beings is not everything. There is a hint of the everlasting in the vastness of the sea."[4] That hint may well be the reason I crave the rustling roll and the murmuring crash, I think; if the Everlasting still hovers over the face of the waters, his voice through them is at once a voice of peace and of summons to me.

Hills and mountains, similarly, can kindle Homeward longing. In *These Happy Golden Years*, Laura Ingalls Wilder remembers stopping on a walk and seeing the Wessington Hills "looking like a blue cloud on the horizon,"[5] which stirs up a desire within her:

---

4. J. B. Phillips, *For This Day: 365 Meditations by J. B. Phillips,* ed. Denis Duncan (Waco, TX: Word Books, 1974), 137–38.

5. Laura Ingalls Wilder, *These Happy Golden Years* (New York: Harper and Row, 1943), 153.

"They are so beautiful that they make me want to go to them," Laura said once.

"Oh, I don't know," Ida replied. "When you got there, they would be just hills, covered with ordinary buffalo grass like this," and she kicked at a tuft of the grass where the green of spring was showing through last year's dead blades.

In a way, that was true; and in another way, it wasn't. Laura could not say what she meant, but to her the Wessington Hills were more than grassy hills. Their shadowy outlines drew her with the lure of far places. They were the essence of a dream. . . . [H]ow mysterious their vague shadow was against the blue sky, far away across miles after miles of green, rolling prairie. She wanted to travel on and on, over those miles, and see what lay beyond the hills.[6]

The beauty of the hills calls Laura both to and beyond themselves. On a recent road trip, I had the odd experience of being able to answer that call in a crude fashion, glimpsing one rise beside the highway in the distance, reaching it, and seeing another down the road. But though we passed thousands of miles of hilltops and the settled or wild valleys in between them, the call never abated. Mystery and the possibility of newness still sang from the next hill.

I hear the same beckoning song in the formation of wild Canada geese in autumn. "The other day I heard the first Canada

---

6. Wilder, *These Happy Golden Years*, 153.

geese go over as I was planting," Tasha Tudor said once. "Their calls give me such a primordial feeling."[7] I can't help straightening up to watch them myself whenever they fly over our own house and garden; their honks are brisk and bracing, like a message from home driven before impending winds of change.

Lastly, music itself sometimes delivers the same indescribable spark. Certain measures have imprinted themselves permanently in my mind with their quickening beauty: Gustav Holst's Thaxted tune, from the middle of his "Jupiter, the Bringer of Jollity" movement in *The Planets*; the stately theme from Aaron Copland's "Appalachian Spring"; the second movement of Dvorak's *New World Symphony*; the alleluia portion of Morten Lauridsen's "O Magnum Mysterium"; the reverent melody of Thomas Newman's "Valley of the Shadow." They seem to speak a wordless language that spells out, in a way no current tongue can, the magnificent, resolute, humble, patient, and ultimately triumphant nature of *hope*.

Taken together, all these motifs stand out like silver whistles that have often blown a tune of Homeward air my way. Seeing their impact in others' lives and my own has led me to ponder their role and presence in the new creation. Why do these elements— sea, hills, autumn geese, music, trees, light, and others—turn up so frequently, in so many places?

I sometimes wonder, with a child's open-ended speculation, if these triggers of Homeward longing are hints of fuller, tangible features—if a part of us instinctively embraces these common factors in current creation because they are integral parts of the

---

7. Tasha Tudor and Richard Brown, *The Private World of Tasha Tudor* (Boston: Little, Brown, 1992), 78.

Home to which we belong. Does music in its most captivating form foreshadow a certain fullness and harmony that our voices will have as we speak with and sing to our Creator? Do we cherish the warm diffused light of the low sideways sun because our souls anticipate the day when the lamp of the New Jerusalem— the Lamb of God, whose glory will render both sun and moon unnecessary (Rev. 21:23)—will dwell with us and beside us?

Putting a young, redeemed imagination to work in this way has been a good exercise for me, especially after the many years in which I thought the Christian life was primarily about avoiding hell. The life motifs above have continually escorted me beyond a mere desire to escape from a burning ship; they have taken me by the hand and led me upward into a kingdom. Bavinck gestures toward the breathtaking array of connections we can make between what is and what shall be:

> The substance [of the city of God] is present in this creation. Just as the caterpillar becomes the butterfly, as carbon is converted into diamond, as the grain of wheat, upon dying in the ground, produces other grains of wheat, as all of nature revives in the spring and dresses up in celebrative clothing, as the believing community is formed out of Adam's fallen race, as the resurrection body is raised from the body that is dead and buried in the earth, so, too, by the re-creating power of Christ, the new heaven and the new earth will one day emerge from the fire-purged elements of this world, radiant in enduring glory and forever set free from the bondage of decay (*douleias*

tēs phthoras). More glorious than this beautiful earth, more glorious than the earthly Jerusalem, more glorious even than Paradise will be the glory of the new Jerusalem whose architect and builder is God himself. The state of glory (*status gloriae*) will be no mere restoration (*restauratie*) of the state of nature (*status naturae*), but a reformation which, thanks to the power of Christ, transforms all matter (*hylē*) into form (*eidos*), all potency into actuality (*potential, actus*), and presents the entire creation before the face of God, brilliant in unfading splendor and blossoming in a springtime of eternal youth.[8]

The reality that awaits us in the New Jerusalem is, as the title of a book by Nancy Guthrie states, *Even Better Than Eden*. As I grasp what I can of the substance of the coming splendor that is scattered through this world, I realize how likely I am to be endlessly astonished in the next.

I am grateful, therefore, for the freedom I've been offered by authors, poets, songwriters, visual artists, and some theologians to broach the possibilities of the new creation. Their explorations have widened my capacity to value beauty and myth, mercy and compassion, love and justice, and majesty. To contemplate what it will be like to live where God works through our work, blessing it into fullness.

---

8. Herman Bavinck, *The Last Things: Hope for This World and the Next,* ed. John Bolt, trans. John Vriend (Grand Rapids: Baker Books, 1996), 160.

Yet, more and more, those explorations are also leading me to hold my imaginings loosely. I find that I don't want to cling to long-cherished depictions that were only ever meant, in their best capacity, to point me forward. Even as I give thanks for valiant fictional characters who have prepared me for my Home, I also want to anticipate meeting heroes who lived quiet and faithful lives; I want the city I long for—perhaps the first city I will ever love—to be more than a pleasing figment of my own devising.

For while my foreknowledge is incomplete, the world to come is by no means nebulous. It is a real place, defined not by my wishes but by its Architect and Builder (Heb. 11:10 NIV). "[T]he newness of new creation is *not arbitrary or capricious*," Jeremy Begbie writes: "New creation does not operate in a sea of infinite possibility."[9] So I am bound to be surprised, to some degree, and bound to find things in it that are as strange as certain aspects of the present world.

Tish Harrison Warren confesses, "I cannot even imagine living with [the ancient Christian] view of the universe, where you can spin around on an average day and bump into a thousand angels. What was assumed for centuries—that the universe is buzzing with divine life—is something I have to stretch to believe."[10] I feel similarly estranged when trying to take in Ezekiel's description of "the whirling wheels" (Ezek. 10:13) that are "full of eyes all around" (v. 12) in Scripture itself, which Madeleine L'Engle

---

9. Jeremy Begbie, "'There Before Us': New Creation in Theology and the Arts," introduction to *The Art of the New Creation: Trajectories in Theology and the Arts,* ed. Jeremy Begbie, Daniel Train, and W. David O. Taylor (Downers Grove, IL: InterVarsity Press, 2022), 15.

10. Tish Harrison Warren, *Prayer in the Night* (Downers Grove, IL: InterVarsity Press, 2021), 83.

borrows to great effect—and my further discomfort—in *A Wind in the Door*. But the solace in the strangeness is the reminder that the God I have come to trust is God; he knows what he is doing, down to the images he chose to give to his prophets in their visions. The further I go, the more thankful I am that he is not a god made by human hands—not a malleable idol who would shape a new heaven and new earth according to my specifications.

I want to arrive, every now and again, at the ends of my imagination. Having come to know Christ in this life, having embraced the signposts, I don't want to miss the final step of readying to relinquish them as I prepare to meet him face-to-face.

"Heaven would not be a homeland if it were not for God being there,"[11] Lynn Anderson states plainly, and Nancy Guthrie speaks for all pilgrims on the Homeward way when she writes: "'Lord, *you* have been our dwelling place in all generations.' We're beginning to understand through this story of the Bible that our longing for home is a longing not for a place but for a person."[12]

Our signposts, motifs, and elements of Homeward longing point us to this Person. To him they will point to the end, calling us to praise, becoming depth markers in our ever-growing understanding of his splendor and majesty.

Meanwhile, I can't help reflecting that even the foreshadowing clues are better than they ought to be.

---

11. Lynn Anderson, *Longing for a Homeland: Discovering the Place You Belong* (West Monroe, LA: Howard, 2004), 167.

12. Nancy Guthrie, *Even Better Than Eden: Nine Ways the Bible's Story Changes Everything about Your Story* (Wheaton, IL: Crossway, 2018), 135.

◇ ◇ ◇

This September evening, the process of preparing dinner bears all the minute thoughtfulness and meaning of a love letter. I don't know why. The windows and doors are wide open to the swan song of the summer leaves. I've washed a cluster of fresh basil—I haven't been able to find it in stores for the past two weeks—and some stems of fresh oregano, and scrubbed a miracle zucchini still warm from the sun. This would be enough to marvel at, really. But I slice open a bell pepper and see the vibrant grain of its inside walls. I notice that every bumblebee cherry tomato from the garden is kissed with the imprint of a flower under its leaves, and all of these come together into something more than gratitude: delight and wonder and a solemn near-bashfulness at receiving this much beauty.

For the first time, I think I don't want to be told any more about heaven and the new creation for the time being. In reading and researching I've often wanted to know just a bit more from Scripture, a little more of a glimpse so that I can be sure of finding high hills or beloved animals or Niggle's Tree in that wide expanse. But perhaps there is even more to our Lord's comparative silence than an encouragement to us to focus faithfully on our work here and now. Perhaps it is also like the mirthful hush of a parent before Christmas morning. It would be like him, I believe.

At any rate, I almost say out loud that I don't want to be told more details in advance—so that when I have seen him face-to-face, I can go among the undying, renewed things one blade of grass, one healing leaf, one ripened fruit at a time, and turn to him, heart and senses shot through with amazement, and say, "You made this, too?"

I am already saying it here.

As I finish cooking, I hear a call, keen and clear, cutting across the cornflower sky. I step over to the back door in time to see three flocks of wild geese pass directly over the garden.

And I laugh a quiet laugh of sheer overwhelm, which is perhaps the closest I've come to the melody of grace.

16

While Hemmed In

As I write, the sun is slipping over the rim of Pikes Peak. In about three and a half hours it will rise over the wheat fields and vineyards of Tuscany, and a short while later gild the stone walls of Beatrix Potter's Hill Top Farm in the United Kingdom. Someday I'd like to be in those places to see that first light.

I am fascinated by travelogues, food writing, expatriate memoirs, and cookbooks. I linger over their well-placed adjectives and concrete nouns, their self-effacing stories of culture shock and unashamed paeans to family recipes. The best of these books refuse to let their descriptions become more sumptuous than their focus on the subject; they teach me to sense the world differently through something as simple as an author's childhood ties to food or a photographer's depiction of light chiseling across local alleys. Through these genres, I've come to appreciate the perspective of writers who exuberantly describe this regional landmark or that process of intricate creation. Above all, I enjoy their tendency to approach new experiences *with the intent to love them*; this stance of expectation makes all the difference in a constantly changing world.

In *The Wind in the Willows*, the Water Rat meets a wayfarer from Constantinople. The stranger spreads a repast of personal adventures and far-flung atmospheres as they break French bread and garlicky sausage together. His stories draw the Water Rat into the jeweled waters of the Adriatic Sea, the tranquil olive woods of Corsica, and the succulent savor of shellfish in Marseilles. Under their spell, Ratty seems borne aloft on the "ballad of the fisherman hauling his nets at sundown against an apricot sky" and "the hungry complaint of the gulls and the sea-mews, the soft thunder of the breaking wave, the cry of the protesting shingle."[1]

I know the feeling. Through tales told by attentive authors, I have listened, enthralled, to the wild percussion of stormy waters on the shores of Prince Edward Island; I've tasted the first spoonful of cold-pressed olive oil in the province of Siena and heard the signal of a metal detector over an ancient Roman treasure trove in Hoxne, England. The generosity of others in lending their eyes and ears allows me to imagine in color, and sketching out the dream of visiting these places is an excursion in joy itself.

Yet when the last wind of whimsy brings me back to my desk and chair, I become aware of my limitations again.

Travel, of course, isn't as simple as packing a bag and stepping out the door; schedules and commitments and budgets must be consulted. These days my body does not easily tolerate acute outdoor heat or intense exercise, so I wonder how far a walk in Cumbria would take me. And since I am, at present, advised

---

1. Kenneth Grahame, *The Wind in the Willows* (New York: Charles Scribner's Sons, 1908), 183.

to avoid caffeine, alcohol, refined carbohydrates, and of course eggs, the sheer existence of tiramisu and the entire country of Italy seems a hilarious and delectable irony. The adventure that shimmers abroad seems to vanish out of reach with these considerations, and I am tempted to resign myself to the bounds of my ordinary life with a sigh.

More often than not, however, I remember a small revelation that occurred a few years ago.

In the middle of some research, I had scanned over the transcript of a panel discussion from a conference. All at once I realized how unlikely it was that I'd ever hold a place at that particular table. They were all pastors and theologians, for one. All men, for another. And for one short, startling moment, I felt stifled. I held no resentment toward the speakers; the pang was more of a fleeting wistfulness born of the fact that I wouldn't naturally fit in with that group because of our differences in profession, geographical location, phase of life, gender, ethnicity, and a dozen other categories.

Yet, as I put down the transcript, the sting faded like a curl of smoke in open air as I looked at what I'd been given in the circle of my life.

That summer I had been waking up to the sight of our garden and thinking about a phrase from Psalm 139: "You hem me in, behind and before" (v. 5). The Hebrew word for "hem" isn't exactly a comforting one; it evokes the image of being under siege, of one who is beset on every side with no escape. Oh, I could see that our little house and garden were decidedly hemmed in. Bordered by wooden privacy fences on all sides, with a refractory slope that stunted plant growth and made outdoor games hard to play, the space at times prompted me to peruse real estate listings that lay beyond our means.

But when the wind whistled softly like a secret keeper in the aspen trees, I looked out and saw the garden for the shelter that it was.

Somehow our yard was the only one on the block to have its own verdant, dappling hedge of trees. The trees themselves weren't even ours; they belonged to our neighbors, which afforded us more planting space for our garden. I had never even thought to wish for such an arrangement when we were looking at houses, but I couldn't help reflecting afterward that my Father *knew*. He knew that I would have to relearn to inhale and exhale in the protected solace of this garden, knew that someday I'd laugh to myself over the dramatic yarns my daughters spun as they tromped between vegetables and flowers and back again in their garden boots. In the safety of this space, the four of us wept and whispered prayers; we laughed aloud and shushed one another with mirth brimming in our eyes; we raised glasses with friends and talked long into the shadows of evening.

He had hemmed us in, behind and before, and within those solid wood-planked boundaries, I saw another truth from the Psalms illustrated clearly before me: "The lines have fallen for me in pleasant places" (16:6). Outside my window I watched black swallowtail butterflies winging and dipping their way between airstreams, stopping only to flutter madly as they laid batches of eggs on the parsley. At dusk I saw a hundred cosmos blossoms radiating palely upon their shadowy stems, like constellations of petals suspended in midair. The pleasantness of the place was derived not from specific material things—those were at my Lord's disposal to give or take away at any time—but from what they signaled about the presence and protection of the Giver. Could the restrictions elsewhere in my life be similar?

I knew that being aware of my own limits didn't mean holding a subdued and cowed posture toward my life or the challenges in it. Every life has some boundaries that should justly be labored against, some that can be embraced, and some that must simply be grieved. But perhaps I could also hold the limitations of the present moment without needing to wait for resolution in every area; I could look at the setting I'd been given in which to "work out the salvation that God [had] given [me]" (Phil. 2:12 PHILLIPS)— my background and personal history, my physical condition, the twenty-four hours before me—and be aware that, above all, I was beset on all sides by the One who loved me most. No matter how small or great my space might be in any given season, there was room to do what he had given me to do.

There was even room to contribute to its beauty.

These days I step out into the garden with secateurs before dinner. My boots search for safe landing spots between plants, but it is a challenge; now that the sloped ground is terraced, everything finds a roothold. Volunteer chamomile fronds and marigold seedlings are still popping up in late September, while the David Austin roses on the top row are throwing an unprecedented fete of glorious peach and ivory blooms. The rest of the garden is purple and white and orange-gold and magenta and pale pink and cream-yellow in these last weeks of the growing season.

This afternoon, rain is streaking down in the distance with an occasional veined flash, and I have barely enough time to cut a pattypan squash and dash back inside. In the kitchen I rinse the scalloped edges with care, cut off the stalk, and prepare the squash for roasting. It won't need much seasoning; when the pale green slices come out of the oven, they will be a buttery, velvety side dish for tonight's rainbow trout.

I like to think I would have ventured to grow (or try) less familiar vegetables if I didn't have dietary restrictions, but I'm quite sure this isn't true. I branched out from the need to break the monotony of run-of-the-mill salads. Yet in the process, unforgettable combinations have landed on our table: black garlic pesto and spaghetti squash, delicata half-moons roasted with butter and cinnamon, Belgian endives filled with curried chicken salad and dotted with fresh blueberries and shredded carrots. I've become increasingly grateful that *vegetables*, in their wide and wild variety, make up a good portion of the eating guidelines for most health conditions. A diet that revolved around something else, like daily quotas of cake or pork belly, would be far less appealing in the long run.

Likewise, though it's harder for me to admit, many strange and rich discoveries have come out of other constraints. A foundational camaraderie exists between strangers who suffer the same ongoing burden or carry similar griefs, and listening to others has increased my understanding of humanity and my well of compassion. I've witnessed the guidance of the Holy Spirit both through the strong, distilled truths of hymns and through the steps of talk therapy; and I would never have believed, until I saw it for myself, that he could bring cheer and *laughter* in the darkest midnight hours. Lately the attitude of L. M. Montgomery's Captain Jim brings a smile, reminding me of the limits of my limits:

> I've kind of contracted a habit of enj'ying
> things. . . . It's got so chronic that I believe I
> even enj'y the disagreeable things. It's great fun
> thinking they can't last. "Old rheumatiz," says I,
> when it grips me hard, "you've *got* to stop aching
> sometime. The worse you are the sooner you'll
> stop, mebbe. I'm bound to get the better of you
> in the long run whether in the body or out of
> the body."[2]

Such surprises are strewn everywhere. They are teaching me to
reassess what I have and what it means to live fully.

Isn't it remarkable? I marvel, occasionally. *Isn't it extraordinary
that each bounded part of this little life can still yield fresh gifts?*

One day the limitations of this world and its entropy and its
societies will drop away for good. But I wonder now if I could
truly recognize the richness in each square inch of the new creation had I not first seen what God is doing in my enclosed spaces
here. Like a British farm field whose layers yield Roman gold and
silver and humus besides, my experience of life on this earth has
little to do with how far I can travel.

One autumn night, I lower a book to my lap as I think back
on the day, unusually alive to its mercies. For an instant, I imagine
what it would be like to embark on a (fully funded) international
research tour of teahouses, cultural legacies, and independent
bookshops. I would love to find a personally meaningful treasure
tucked away in the back shelves of an antiques booth or chat with

---

2. L. M. Montgomery, *Anne's House of Dreams* (Toronto: McClelland and
Stewart, 1922), 130–32.

a host whose family has lived in the same village for generations. But in between constantly unpacking and repacking suitcases, funneling through security lines, missing friends with whom I want to share the experience, and enduring the inevitable headaches and fatigue and chaos which come with travel, it's possible I would end up dreaming of a small house, perhaps in the vicinity of tall mountains, with a fenced-in cottage garden where one could raise vegetables with a small family. Of a quiet life where I could see Christ's power being perfected in my weakness (2 Cor. 12:9) and where I could learn what it means to abide in the awareness that he is my Bread of Life, my Living Water, my daily sufficient grace.

How much there is yet to taste and behold and explore here between these borderlines. I can scarcely guess how much more I will uncover in the time that I have. With him, I'm ready for tomorrow's dawn to break.

17

Along Winding Paths

We are in an enchanted place. On a whim, the four of us have ventured into a volunteer-run botanic garden in early spring, and my senses—startled to full attention after the first step inside the gate—are completely satiated. So far I've supped on the lazuline shades of Muscari blossoms and the ambrosial air of crab apple and chokecherry trees. I've sampled the vivacity of white phlox star-blooms that are tumbling out of their beds in an impish riot; how could there be more?

Slim, earthy paths branch off the main walkways. They lead us under cathedral-height tree limbs and into patches of sunlit perennials that shimmer like jewel collections displayed with no heed for lock and key.

I listen, content, to the andante crunch of grit under my shoes. The girls fly ahead, and suddenly they are back again, asking if we can please walk the secret trail.

"How did you find it?" I ask. They speed me over to a bench, just past multiple signs that forbid any climbing of the rocks, to a small plaque on the ground that announces:

Secret Trail
Warning

Large Rocks

Difficult Trail

Its cheekiness makes me grin. We follow the "secret, difficult trail" single file onto a low ledge of small boulders and into a shadowy tunnel of trees. The tunnel isn't long, and soon it opens out into a shaded spot overseen by a metal eagle high atop a slender trunk.

Following another avenue that winds back to a wider lane, I think of the first time I recognized that God's priorities regarding paths were different from mine. I was in my early twenties and eager to move on to the next adventure in my life—if only I could figure out what it was. The matter of marriage was particularly perplexing. Surely it was possible for the Almighty to shine a flashlight into the distance so I could see ahead and make my way to the place where I was supposed to be.

Then I tripped over the truth rooted in Psalm 119:105: "Your word is a lamp to my feet and a light to my path." A lamp was not what I wanted at that juncture. I wanted more than a bright circle around my feet that provided only enough illumination for the next step and then the next. Yet this did not seem to be the way of the God of Joseph, the God of Esther, the God of the pillars of cloud and flame in the desert. Slowly it sank in that God wasn't focused on simply getting me from point A to point B; he was focused on the person I was going to be by the time I reached point B. It seemed that the efficiency of the trip mattered little compared to the transformation of the traveler and her dependence on her Guide.

Somewhat older now, I see the same pattern in the broader scope of the road Home. Now that I have come in the sheepfold door (John 10:9), there remains the monumental, God-sized task of fitting me for the life ahead. The journey of the Homeward pilgrim is not merely one to be endured; it is one that is meant to prepare us for Home, so to speak, as much as Home is being prepared for us.

To be clear, it isn't that we must be made into people who are deemed worthy of love. That gift, bestowed freely, has arrived already. But the God who is perfect Love (1 John 4:8, 16–17), as I learned from Thomas Traherne, has a vision more compelling than letting us be:

> Love can forbear, and Love can forgive. . . . But Love can never be reconciled to an unlovely object. . . . He can never therefore be reconciled to your sin, because sin itself is incapable of being altered: but He may be reconciled to your person, because that may be restored: and, which is an infinite wonder, to greater beauty and splendour than before.[1]

---

1. Thomas Traherne, *Centuries* (Brooklyn, NY: Angelico, 2020), 71–72. The quotation is from the Second Century, meditation 30. Readers of Lewis's *The Problem of Pain* may recognize the first part of this quotation from one of the chapter mottoes. These lines have been one of the most enduring legacies of that book to me, probably because it was the first time I encountered the notion that Love, if Love were indeed perfect and real and personified, could not leave me in the state he found me.

His view reaches to depths and lengths farther than we can fathom, and his plan takes into account the person he created each one of us to be. "The purpose of God's salvation," Keller writes, "is that we be 'conformed to the image of his Son' (Rom. 8:29)."[2] Such conformation doesn't mean we shall be clones but individual sons and daughters who share Christ's glory as a resurrected people, each bearing his unclouded image in a distinct way for eternity.

Meanwhile, the work of that transformation is underway, but it is not finished yet.

Along the track of recent years, as gray and jagged as the stones that mottle the path under my feet, the uglier parts of myself have become more apparent to me. My skepticism. My insecurities. My selfishness when presented with inconvenient opportunities to help others who are in greater need or constant suffering. I wish I could unsee the hurt I've caused by cherishing assumptions about other people or by being unkind to my own family, except I also wish I could keep it pinned in my peripheral vision to keep myself from repeating the pattern.

I have not asked the questions the people around me needed to be asked.

I have rarely viewed them as they ought to be viewed.

Many of these realizations, indeed, have to do with the help I have withheld from and the hurt I have inflicted upon others. These days I often think about a poem by Anne Porter called "A Short Testament," and find myself echoing its themes in prayer. *Where I have spoken or acted wrongly, and so contributed in some measure to the death and not to the life of another, forgive me. Show*

---

2. Timothy Keller, *Hope in Times of Fear: The Resurrection and the Meaning of Easter* (New York: Viking, 2021), 124.

me how to right it. Mend what I cannot, with an abundance I cannot fathom. If I have not loved them—ah, I have not loved him.

In a way, the timing of this soberness is unexpected. Some knowledge of my sins and weaknesses decades ago made me want to accept Christ's rescue and give him my life, but a different, keener awareness makes me step aside more willingly to let him do his work in me now.

A few years ago, an Anglican priest led a service of blessing for an artists' retreat I attended. He invited us into a time of confession and repentance in prayer by saying, "Come lay your sins down, and ask for his forgiveness. You don't have to carry them anymore." Since that day I have never been able to think of confession the way I used to, as the duty of "owning up" to all my faults and flaws under a watchful eye. The throne of grace invites me to come near to receive mercy (Heb. 4:16) and breathe freely again. I am like a patient who finally understands that a dreaded diagnosis itself does not bring doom but reveals a trouble that was already underway; confession, like that diagnosis, is an acknowledgment of a current state of need. What I need is healing, and the freedom of a clear heart, and relief. The further I go, the more I want to shed the old self, despite all it may take to get there.

"I have been crucified with Christ. It is no longer I who live, but Christ who lives in me. And the life I now live in the flesh I live by faith in the Son of God, who loved me and gave himself for me" (Gal. 2:20), Paul writes. The littler deaths that necessarily follow this change of life are still hard—the ones that call for reconciliation, repentance, endurance, and surrender. They are the work of a lifetime.

With this in mind, I've sometimes pictured analogies for what it will be like to come Home to the Lord. In one, the long-awaited sound of his voice cuts through the predawn air over a field where I and others are laboring, followed by a pause. Shovels clank to the earth. A handful of seeds, mid-scatter, showers haphazardly down, and saltwater stains a limping trail of steps into everlasting arms.

Perhaps it will be like that. I do not think John would tell us that God "will wipe away every tear from [our] eyes" (Rev. 21:4) if it were not so.

◇ ◇ ◇

Just past the eagle sculpture in the botanic park, a thin ribbon of a trail drops down a flight of wooden steps. On this first visit, I am disoriented by the many loops and lines that lattice the place, and I nearly turn back. What benefit can there be to going further on this particular path, which appears to skirt the wooded edge of the park? What notable feature could possibly lie this way besides an unhindered stretch of chain-link fence and possibly the restrooms?

Yongwon emerges into view, walking toward me. "Go on," he says. "You'll want to see this."

I turn the corner and gasp.

A thick carpet of blue Muscari runs from the edge of the path into a crowd of daffodils and tulips, canopied by trees flowering from branch to branch in strawberries and cream. A few of the tulips are flamboyant in yellow with flames of red imprinted on their sides; behind them nod more cupped blossoms in crimson, orange, soft violet, and white. Only in the plant realm could these hues look so marvelous together, I think. Mixed with the dappling midday sun, the whole sight is a balm for the soul. Here are the heralds of the green and growing season, though they themselves have taken time to reach this point. In the dim days of snow and frost, some message beckoned them to climb upward, inch by arduous inch, loaded with precious cargo.

The effect is so deliciously lush and kaleidoscopic that I forget how long we've been on our feet and all the sinuous routes we took to get here; I circle the bed, crouch down to greet the crinkling smiles of tiny violas, stand back up to gaze overhead, and forget the time altogether. What can hold a candle to the jubilance of this array? Other spectators have gathered about it with their phones and cameras as well, and we gaze from various angles without jostling one another, like honeybees clustered on ripe peaches. If we come back in later years—I decide on the spot—we must come here, to this radiant showcase of early spring, where these flowers bloom as if they *know* death has been conquered forever and the age of rejoicing must continue apace.

Perhaps it will be like this, too.

18

With Bluets

I am at my computer, lost down a rabbit trail of research for a conference talk, when the photograph strikes.

Stapled papers and books around me are sprawled open to passages about Sehnsucht and the vulnerable music, poetry, and prose that have been written on the subject. Immersing myself in the accounts of others sometimes makes me forget my own, and in a brief moment of doubt, I hope I am not shoehorning my life into a construct that isn't really true of it.

I think again of the words C. S. Lewis wrote to Mary Van Deusen: "The new photos raise extreme *Sehnsucht*: each a landscape as fulfils [*sic*] my dreams. *That* is the America I wd. [*sic*] like to see, not the great cities, which, except superficially, are really much the same all over the earth."[1] The photos were likely of a

---

1. Lewis to Mary Van Deusen, June 6, 1952, *The Collected Letters of C. S. Lewis, Vol. III: Narnia, Cambridge and Joy, 1950–1963* (New York: HarperCollins, 2007), 199.

region not too far from where I grew up, and I want to see if I can give a sense of the environs.

On a stock photo site, I search for images of "Blue Ridge," "Boone," and—after a minute's recollection—"Grandfather Mountain," a local natural landmark. The craggy outline of an old man's face against the sky, taken from different angles and seasons, makes me smile.

As I scroll, a vivid image of a patch of tiny blue astral blossoms springs up on the screen. Bluets.

I blink.

In a twinkling, I am eight years old again in the Kellwood valley, kneeling beside clusters of these miniature stars that have scattered themselves along the brook on threadlike stems.

I am twelve, shyly answering a guest speaker's question during a chapel service in Seoul when he calls on me.

"What's your favorite flower?"

"Bluets."

"Bluets! There's one I've never heard of. What are they?"

"They're . . . a small blue flower."

"All right then," he says, turning back to the rest of the room, "we've got roses and daisies and 'bluets, a small blue flower' in the garden we're imagining. Now, I want you to close your eyes and walk along these rows of color."

I am a bride, holding the satin-wrapped stems of blue hydrangeas and ivory calla lilies in one hand and the interlacing clasp of my husband's fingers in the other.

I am lagging behind my family at the botanic park, bewildered by the impossible, almost electric shade of the blue gentians.

And, finally, I am kneeling in my garden, sowing seeds that promise blooms the color of the untrammeled sky for the umpteenth time. Master gardeners and plant nurseries tell me that true blues are rare in the botanical realm, and by this point I know this firsthand. Even the bluets I remember tend toward pale lavender, though I remember some that lived up to their name. Our Blue Victory salvia comes up in undeniably purple spires every year. The Endless Summer hydrangea that survived for one summer insisted on blushing a rosy pink in spite of the soil acidifier I mixed around its base, and our Siberian Blues dianthus has flourished into a veritable cloud of shocking magenta. Other attempts have stopped short of fruition—such as the forget-me-nots I tried many springs ago that never germinated, and the heliotrope that stayed confined to its packet due to the toxins it would bring to our child-friendly garden—but the genuinely blue countenances of creeping speedwell and *linum perenne* flax cheer me every spring.

"What is it that gives bluebells their particular enchantment?" Malcolm Guite asks, surveying "shimmering pools" of those flowers in his home country of England.[2] It isn't merely their heralding of spring, he decides:

> It is more than that: it is the colour itself; for it is the colour of the sky, suddenly come down to earth. When we look up into that enticing blue, it always escapes us, always recedes; it is everywhere and nowhere. However high we fly,

---

2. Malcolm Guite, *In Every Corner Sing: A Poet's Corner Collection* (Norwich: Canterbury Press, 2018), 134.

the blue is always beyond us; but, here, in these
secret scatterings and holy showings deep in the
woods, that blue is on our level, beckoning us to
look down as well as up, and to take off our shoes
on holy ground.[3, 4]

For decades, I have chased blue flowers without seeing the pattern
of my pursuit. But in this moment and this context, I recall that
C. S. Lewis declared himself a "votary of the blue flower" in his
spiritual autobiography.[5] Alan Jacobs succinctly traces the background of this phrase:

[Lewis] is thinking of Novalis—the pen name
of the German Romantic writer Friedrich von
Hardenberg, who died in 1801 at the age of
twenty-nine. The protagonist of Novalis's unfinished allegorical novel *Heinrich Von Ofterdingen*
becomes obsessed by a vision of a blue flower,
which he first encounters in a stranger's tales and
then in dreams. . . .

---

3. Guite, *In Every Corner Sing*, 134–35.

4. Tracing the history of human recognition of the color, James Fox con-
curs: "Blue, in short, is the most elusive of colors. It slips through our fingers
and retreats just as fast as we approach it. That may be why, as the poet Robert
Frost once observed, we 'wish for blue.' We wish for it because we know we
can't have it" (James Fox, *The World According to Color: A Cultural History*
[New York: St. Martin's, 2021], 114).

5. C. S. Lewis, *Surprised by Joy: The Shape of My Early Life* (San Diego:
Harcourt Brace, 1955), 7.

> [Von Ofterdingen] "yearns" or "longs" (*sehn*)
> for the flower—and yet nothing that he can grasp
> seems so desirable as that longing itself.[6]

Thus the blue flower is a symbol for Sehnsucht, always drawing its seekers forward to something that is not itself.

Before me now is this photograph of my own familiar blue flowers, found while retracing the steps where Homeward longing has led me. The photographer himself doesn't know what they are called; I would not have stumbled across this snapshot if I had not been looking back in this particular way today. Thus, with the review of Sehnsucht fresh in my mind and the long corridor of blue flowers open in my memory, I turn back and perceive a thriving trail of evidence I did not expect.

God has been waiting at the end of my search all along. Before I walked up the hill to the meadow, before I ever read or heard of Lewis or German Romanticism, before I crossed the Pacific Ocean or the borders of Middle-earth or the waiting rooms of specialist clinics, he was at the beginning, present in the small ways I could comprehend, as low and near as blue cross-shaped flowers at my eye-level beside a running rill.

He was, for that child, what he is for all who ache with a Homeward longing: the answer given before we even know the questions that voice our need. "All the days ordained for me were written in your book before one of them came to be" (Ps. 139:16 NIV), as King David writes. Long has our Lord planned the end

---

6. Alan Jacobs, *The Narnian: The Life and Imagination of C. S. Lewis* (New York: HarperOne, 2005), 40–41.

of our story, becoming the crux of our new life "while we were powerless to help ourselves" (Rom. 5:6 PHILLIPS).

The search of Homeward longing is, in the end, an unfolding of layer after layer of the mercy and involvement and character of God. Like the blue that startles us at our feet and casts our gaze upward to the blue that arches overhead, his love surrounds us until we notice it anew and murmur aloud with recognition and amazed exaltation:

"All this time."

Epilogue

A steady drizzle of summer rain coats the brick sidewalks and cobblestone streets, turning the light from the streetlamps into blurry golden moons on the ground. On this early evening, The Grey Lady, otherwise known as Nantucket Island, seems ready to wrap herself in a thick coverlet of her signature fog and settle in for the night. Two figures under tilted umbrellas walk by storefronts and small gardens, stopping to admire the effect of blue hydrangeas against gray-and-white cottages. They move at a pace befitting two people on their honeymoon.

Yongwon is keeping track of where and how far we've walked with a handheld GPS, foreshadowing future years of keeping his old-fashioned wife up-to-date with technology. At the end of each day, he shows me the squiggles we've etched all over the small town, and I smile at both our differences and the evidence of our easygoing adventures together.

New places still load me with trepidation sometimes, but this trip feels different. I have never traveled to an unfamiliar place with Yongwon before, and I watch the way he explores his immediate surroundings, the way he magically compacts items into his sling backpack. Observing him takes some of the edge off my alertness, which helps me feel less out of place. But it is mainly his company that frees me to embrace this experience and notice nearby details without feeling overwhelmed.

We ramble down side streets, reading cottage names off of their quarter boards. Sweet Pea. Fairwinds. He points out green shutters that have miniature ships cut out of their corners. At the whaling museum, I read aloud to him from the perfect penmanship of a captain's log. We purchase chocolate-covered cranberries, linger to watch the shaping of handmade ice cream cones at the smoothie shop, and stoop to admire water meter covers on the road that have the island's outline stamped on them. On the night we dress up for dinner, a bow-tied waiter passes us on our way into the restaurant and remarks, in a gentle accent I wish I could place, "*Oh, erregant,*" paying the compliment with such kindness that I glow like a firefly for a few seconds.

As the tiny, deafening plane takes off on the last day and banks so that we can see the wing-shaped little island for a final farewell, I carry with me a souvenir that will last a lifetime: the anchored feeling of going somewhere new with someone I love, who loves me well.

◇ ◇ ◇

In recent years, I've felt once again that I am in unfamiliar territory. Worldwide and personal circumstances have left me a little more worn and tattered after each annual bend in the road. At times the journey Home feels interminably long.

But the experience I was privileged to have so many years ago as a newlywed is oddly fresh in my mind as I stumble along beside my Lord. My progress is not elegant. The situations I'm encountering for the first time are hardly the stuff of vacation. But as I look to him amid the uncertainty, I am amazed and grateful to see what he is doing with our time.

For I know now that it is possible to weep with him and then get up and keep going. I'm still surprised by moments that give me a jovial suspicion regarding his sense of humor. With the greatest kindness, he keeps walking me off the ledge of my capabilities so that, it seems, I will stop attempting to live within them. And he has so consistently been my wild card of help and peace that I've shed much of the fear I used to keep clutched about my soul. Even when I falter, he fills up the minutes with his patience, the unfolding of everyday eucatastrophes, and the slow work of establishing my roots in joy. Every step taken with him, whether down or up, is a step Homeward.

When these years are finished, I will never again know the experience of having to lean on him in such fallen weakness. But *I will remember it*, when the union between Christ and his church comes into unmarred sweetness. When I see his face for the thousandth time.

And so the ache grows. Always gliding a few steps ahead, it has led me from a rote understanding of my Lord into the careful tread of toeing the line, and from there into the freer movement of a deepening love. I find now that I want not merely to obey but to delight him, more than anything else. Receiving all that he has given and rendering my all back to him in love, as he does the greater work in me: I believe this is, of all things, what it means to live Homeward.

I ask, then, for the grace to do so. And I ask the same for my fellow travelers, wherever their own roads may take them before we come into the beauty and the glory of our King:

> *Strengthen us with your joy.*
>
> *Keep our hearts burning within us at the sound of your voice and the glimmers of the place you are preparing, so that we may sing your song even under a darkling sky and be glad.*
>
> *Walk us Home.*

Acknowledgments

This book is not one I would have—or could have—written ten years ago. Writing it has been like watching the improbable growth of a tree in the barren wild, and I am deeply grateful to the many people who have made its existence possible.

Anita Palmer somehow believed in this book when it was a mere sprout. Don Pape found hospitable shelter for it, and his unflagging encouragement and wise counsel as an agent were vital in bringing it to maturity. Kimberlee Ireton, Pastor Kevin Boaz, and Rachel Boaz were the first readers to look the manuscript over from top to bottom; I am indebted to them for helping me grasp what to nurture and what to prune.

I could not have found this book a better editor than Ashley Gorman, so I am glad such coordination was out of my hands; her comments and guidance not only helped strengthen the chapters but made me look forward to revising them. Many, many thanks to the design, editorial, and production teams at B&H for their ideas and attention to detail!

Looking further back, I know I could not have completed this work if others had not first faithfully gone about theirs. Thank you to:

Lancia Smith, whose cultivation of artist Christians is the longest-term investment I have ever witnessed. You gave this writer—and so many others—a place to garner the courage to establish strong roots and to grow upward.

The writers, artists, and musicians at The Cultivating Project, including Matthew Clark, Amy Malskeit, Leslie Bustard, Kris Camealy, Adam Nettesheim, Gianna Soderstrom, and Terri Moon. Your generous creativity, candidness, and humor fill out the unseen margins of your pieces, and I'm so glad to be in community with you.

Christina and Brian Brown, who have given so much of themselves to Anselm and their other spheres of service. Your hospitality, your gifts, and your perseverance have planted a grove larger and more beautiful than you know.

Every writer, artist, and musician of the Anselm Guild. I would write down all of your names if I could. Thank you for sharing your dreams, challenges, and stories through the years; so many of them have shaped my own for the better.

The Anselm Society community, for listening to many of these ideas in their early stages and letting me know when they resonated with you.

The Rabbit Room community, for your openhearted and vibrant conversations and for making space for creativity and faith to thrive.

I am especially thankful to Esther Yang, my writing partner and Other Half, for her presence and ever-heartening perspective;

to Amanda and Nick Gerber, and Brianna and Chris Curran, for sharing the joys and sorrows of everyday life with us for so many years; and to Chris and Sharon Baik, for listening so thoughtfully to the idea of this book up in the mountains and being people we love to be with.

Mom and Dad, thank you so much for researching all of my questions about family history and cheering me on through every stage. You are a blessing.

Evangeline and Juliet, you have created a stack of stories, poems, and drawings in the time it took me to write one book. How I love talking and laughing with you every day! Your joyful anticipation for the new creation has increased mine, and I hope these chapters do the same for you.

And to Yongwon, who from the beginning invited me to follow the Lord wherever he might lead us: what an adventure it has been, and is. I'm so glad to be traveling this road with you.